Prayers for Men

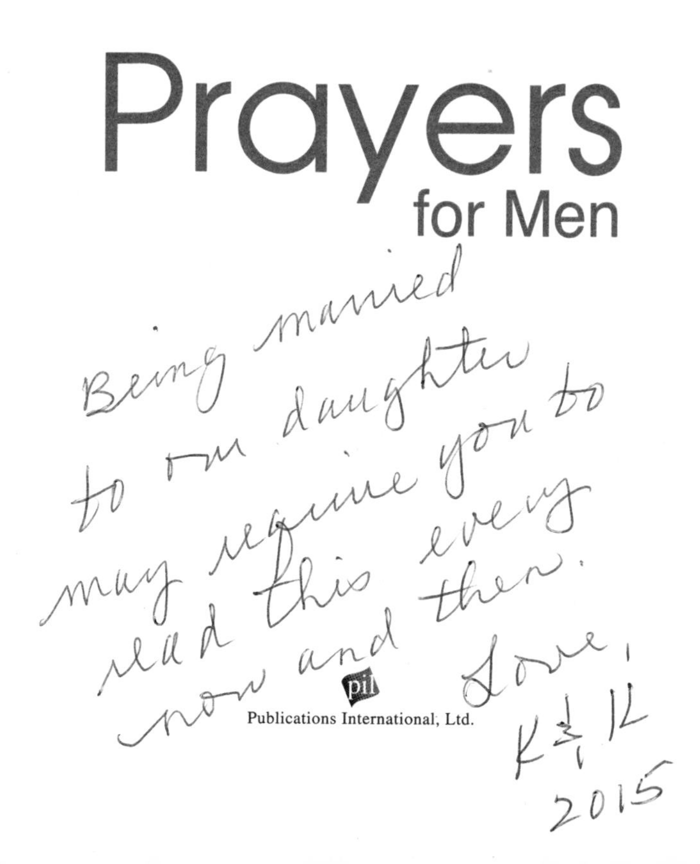

pil
Publications International, Ltd.

Contributing writer: Janice Deal

Interior art: Shutterstock.com

Louis Weber, CEO
Publications International, Ltd.
7373 North Cicero Avenue
Lincolnwood, Illinois 60712

ISBN: 978-1-68022-128-2

Manufactured in China.

8 7 6 5 4 3 2 1

Contents

Prayers for Men offers prayers, Bible verses, and quotations for a broad spectrum of situations and experiences men encounter in life. In straightforward, everyday language, these prayers echo the thoughts and feelings that rise up from a man's heart.

You may choose to read the book in sequence from cover to cover. Or you can select a chapter that best reflects the place in which you find yourself. There are 20 chapters to choose from, with themes such as faith, forgiveness, pride, praise, marriage, parenthood, strength, work and leadership, aging, and heaven.

The prayers in each chapter are intended to help draw you into dialogue with an ever-present, approachable God, who lovingly calls you into companionship. Individual prayers are brief enough to read in a minute or two, but they'll provide food for thought throughout your day.

Whether *Prayers for Men* becomes a permanent treasure on your personal bookshelf or a book passed among friends, you may be blessed in some way by the role it plays in supporting and strengthening your growing relationship with God.

Faith

Know therefore that the Lord thy God, he is God, the faithful God, which keepeth covenant and mercy with them that love him and keep his commandments to a thousand generations.

—Deuteronomy 7:9

Today I found out that a close friend has been diagnosed with pancreatic cancer. Dear God, this man was healthy. He kept fit and he ate a good diet. His family is devastated, and I am reminded of how quickly our lives can change. God, some change makes me afraid, and in the face of my fear, I must remember to have faith in you. I must never lose sight of the fact that you keep the faith for me, also; you are there for me. I can share my fears with you. I can unburden myself. I can ask you how to best support my friend and his loved ones. Dear God, please help me to remember that faith is a two-way street: even as I work to remain faithful to you and all you stand for, you are faithful to me, and I can take comfort in that fact.

Faith and fear cannot coexist. One always gives way to the other. We need to be constantly building up our faith to overcome the numerous sources of destructive disbelief all around us. We must continually work at rekindling the gift of God that is in us, which is our faith in him and in his promises. We need to be dedicated to developing a spirit of love and power and discipline within ourselves. Studying the words of the scriptures, meditating on them, keeping his commandments, and praying daily are some of the ways we can do this. By doing so, we shut out fear and cultivate faith.

Now faith is the substance of things hoped for, the evidence of things not seen.

—Hebrews 11:1

My daughter has a child's Bible, and she loves the stories about Jesus and the miracles he wrought: water into wine, healing the sick. "Dad, why don't we see miracles like this anymore?" she asked me just yesterday. Her question echoed a wish I have had on more than one occasion. Living in a society so bent on flash, on the next best thing, I myself have yearned to see visible signs of God's presence. But as my daughter and I talked, we began to acknowledge the presence of miracles in the everyday: the antibiotic she took last week for an ear infection; the rosemary seeds we'd planted together, which are gaining traction and sprouting up. Health and new life burgeon behind the scenes. Our world is, in fact, full of miracles! And when we cannot recognize them for the miracles they are? Then we must rely on faith. God, help me to see the miracles in my life, and strengthen me to have faith even when I don't see visible signs of your presence.

Almighty God, our faith in you is undergirded by your faithfulness. No matter how many times we turn away, you patiently wait for us to return to you. Instill in us that same sense of honor and faithfulness that is yours, Lord. May we be as faithful to you as you have been to us.

Lord, perfect for me what is lacking of thy gifts; of faith, help thou mine unbelief; of hope, establish my trembling hope; of love, kindle its smoking flax.

—Lancelot Andrewes

My servant Moses is not so,
who is faithful in all mine house.

—Numbers 12:7

I miss my parents, both of whom died within the last 10 years, but each day I strive to keep them alive—in my heart and in the world—by emulating the way they lived their lives. On days when I struggle, I remember my mother's kindness and my father's acts of service. I remember the day my dad and I shared coffee and talked about the qualities he admired in others: "Faith," he said, without hesitation. "Faith in God, in one's own path. From faith springs generosity of spirit." He went on to say that in the Bible, the stories of faith as embodied by men such as Moses uplifted him. Dear God, may I persevere and have faith. Help me to remember that faithfulness is an attribute of great men like Moses, and within my reach as I strive to be my best self.

Dear Jesus, I find myself at the intersection of faith and doubt. I do believe in you, but it's not always easy. I have a lot of questions, a lot of problems, and not very many answers. When I was younger, I had a lot of confidence, but not so much now. Help me, Lord Jesus, in my unbelief. Fan the flickering flame of my faith.

Understanding is the reward of faith.
So do not seek to understand in order to believe,
but believe so that you may understand.

—St. Augustine

Then Ahimelech answered the king, and said, And who is so faithful among all thy servants as David, which is the king's son in law, and goeth at thy bidding, and is honourable in thine house?

—1 Samuel 22:14

I have traditionally thought of faith as a way to keep strong my personal connection to God. But this week I found myself in conversation with a new workmate, an atheist, who asked me point blank whether I believe in God. When I avowed that I do, my companion asked what sustains that conviction, to which I replied simply, "Faith." That night, as I reviewed the conversation, I felt relief that I had made clear my beliefs. To downplay them, I realized, would have felt like a betrayal. In that moment I was struck by the revolutionary idea that God wants us to be faithful simply to serve him. Dear Lord, help me to remember that faith is more than a means of strengthening my relationship with you—it's also a way of serving you.

And brought in the offerings and the tithes and the dedicated things faithfully: over which Cononiah the Levite was ruler, and Shimei his brother was the next.

—2 Chronicles 31:12

Dear God, money is tight this summer: our old refrigerator gave out sooner than we might have hoped and replacing it was an unexpected expense, as was the series of doctor's visits when I strained my shoulder. Last Sunday, the ushers passed the offering plate and I am ashamed to admit that I held back. After all, I justified, I am spread thin this month! Rather than contributing something, I contributed nothing, and in my frugality, I lost both connection and the sense of continuity I strive for in my spiritual life. Lord, giving to you is not only an act of faith (because I am giving to someone unseen), but also something I should do faithfully. Thank you for helping me to remember this.

For therein is the righteousness of God revealed
from faith to faith: as it is written,
The just shall live by faith.

—Romans 1:17

Faith is more than a passive idea; it is a principle of action that motivates our day-to-day decisions and actions. Would a farmer plant if he did not expect to harvest? Would a student read and study if he did not believe it would improve his quality of life? We daily act upon things we believe in even when we can't yet see the end result. We live by this faith, whether we identify it as such or not.

As faithful people, we take this principle one step further. We do things that are motivated by our faith in things promised to us but not yet fulfilled. We smile in the face of adversity. We continue in prayer even when those prayers don't seem to be answered. We stop saying, "I can't" and start believing God can! Step-by-step, we put our faith into action and learn to "live by faith."

Only faith can look past a seemingly impossible situation and believe that it will change. I believe you are a God of miracles, Lord. These are days of miracles, as were the days of Noah, Moses, and Joseph. I may not see the seas parted, peoples freed, or congregations caught up to heaven, but through faith, I expect wonderful gifts from you. I believe that with you, all things are possible!

Faith is a true sign of bravery. It is looking forward to the future despite challenges and adversity; it is trusting in something that you can neither see nor touch yet knowing it is always there guiding you along life's path.

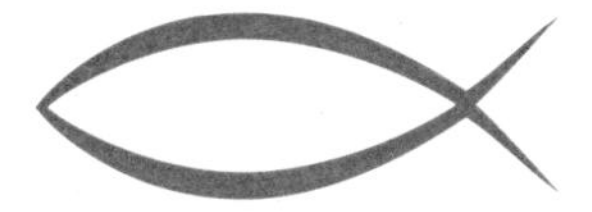

Praise

Let them praise thy great and terrible name;
for it is holy.

—Psalm 99:3

I try not to swear in front of my children, but the other day, while attempting to fix a few loose boards, I hit my thumb, not the fence, with my hammer. I took the Lord's name in vain and howled a few other choice epithets while hopping in pain around the backyard. My two little daughters were playing nearby, which meant I had to do some apologizing after the fact. "Dad spoke God's name in anger—not cool," I began. I explained how a name is a profound thing. "It would feel bad if I yelled your name in an angry way, wouldn't it?" I asked the girls. They nodded their heads vigorously. "God doesn't like it when you yell his name either, does he?" my littlest asked. "God's name is powerful and holy," I said, hugging her. "It should be said with praise." At that point, I decided the fence could wait, and we went out for ice cream. But the conversation stayed with me. Lord, when I say your name, may it always be with the proper reverence.

And hath made us kings and priests unto God and his Father; to him be glory and dominion for ever and ever. Amen.

—Revelation 1:6

I am an editor by trade and a fiction writer by choice. For the past several years, I have been working on a novel in the evening and on weekends. Yesterday I made final touches on what I believe is the final draft. I closed my laptop, pulled on my jacket, and went for a long walk. It was almost hard to believe that the project that has consumed my free time for so long was complete. I felt a strange mix of relief and exhilaration, and experienced a great welling of praise in my heart. Lord, you have been with me every step of the way, even when things seemed unclear as to how to proceed with this book. Now it is done! Thank you, thank you, for being there. Thank you for helping me to accomplish this.

Lord, I pray I will stop taking all your miraculous works for granted. Whether I praise you through song, words, or actions, I want to praise you not only for what you are doing, but also for all you have done in the past. Help me see the holiness of the ordinary in each day.

Give thanks and praise for what you have, and your prayers are already answered.

I will praise the name of God with a song,
and will magnify him with thanksgiving.

—Psalm 69:30

My daughter Alexa, a high school student, loves to sing. She has been involved in choir since she was a little girl. Yesterday was Monday, and my daughter came home from school discouraged about a misunderstanding with a friend, and the fact that she had more homework than she'd anticipated. Every Monday evening is rehearsal time for the church choir Alexa is in. The kids meet for an hour or so to practice right after dinner. Usually she looks forward to it, but yesterday she didn't want to go. She felt tired and worried about her schoolwork. I encouraged her to go anyway, and promised that I'd be right there at the end of practice, ready to bring her back home. When I dropped my girl off, she looked positively glum. Imagine my surprise when I picked up a beaming, transformed daughter an hour later! "I can't believe I always forget how good this choir makes me feel!" Alexa enthused, and I had to smile. Lord, thank you for reminding me and my beloved daughter how praising you in song can uplift one's heart.

But I will hope continually,
and will yet praise thee more and more.

—Psalm 71:14

My old college friend Tom is an artist. He lives in a city near my home, and occasionally he'll have a gallery showing of his work downtown. I always try to make his shows, and we usually also manage to get together for a meal every month or so. His shows are a perfect time for me to compliment his work. But one evening when we were just meeting for dinner, I mentioned how impressed I am by a series of sculptures he's been making from pressed wood. Even though I had already praised that same work at a recent show, the innovative nature of the work has stayed with me, and I wanted to share that. Tom was uplifted by my comment. It turns out he'd had a frustrating day in the studio and my admiration, coming from out of the blue like that, meant a lot to him. The experience reminded me that praise is not a one-time thing—you never know when another person might be struggling, or how much repeating a kind word can mean. God, may I remember to uplift others even as I praise you, again and again.

On our way to rejoicing gladly let us go.
Christ our Lord has conquered; vanquished is the foe.
Christ without, our safety; Christ within, our joy;
who, if we be faithful, can our hope destroy?
On our way rejoicing; as we forward move,
hearken to our praises, O lest God of love!
Unto God the Father joyful songs we sing;
unto God the Savior thankful hearts we bring;
unto God the Spirit bow we and adore,
on our way rejoicing now and evermore.
On our way rejoicing; as we forward move,
hearken to our praises, O blest God of love!

—John S. Monsell

Is any among you afflicted? let him pray.
Is any merry? let him sing psalms.

—James 5:13

In a church or family, praising can have the nice effect of building up others and spreading cheer. In our house, we'll occasionally indulge in what we call "love bombardment." Someone will get singled out for a blitz of praise, during which everyone else in the house heaps compliments upon the designated recipient. We usually focus on someone who's had a long or challenging day. It doesn't take long for everyone to be caught up in laughter, and the object of affection gets a nice boost. Everyone needs a lift sometimes, and taking part in praise bombardment has proven, in our house at least, to be a balm for all concerned. Dear Lord, help me to remember that attitudes are infectious.

How amiable are thy tabernacles, O Lord of hosts!
My soul longeth, yea, even fainteth for the courts
of the Lord: my heart and my flesh crieth out
for the living God. Yea, the sparrow hath
found an house, and the swallow a nest for herself,
where she may lay her young, even thine altars,
O Lord of hosts, my King, and my God.
Blessed are they that dwell in thy house:
they will be still praising thee.

—Psalm 84:1–4

How the writer of this psalm loved to praise God! His longing to be in a place where he could join others in worship made his soul feel faint with desire. To him, even the birds who built their nests near God's altar seemed to be singing praises to their creator.

Lord, I long to join in the praise as well. Fill my heart with a yearning to worship you, O Lord!

Strength

I can do all things through Christ
which strengtheneth me.

—Philippians 4:13

My parents' deaths effected a profound transition for me. My mother died when I was 30 years old, and my father died this year, less than two years after we lost Mom. I am an adult, a single dad, and though I have been self-sufficient for years, I deeply miss being able to call my parents for counsel when faced with life's challenges. Mom and Dad were always there to support me and my son Evan. Since their deaths, I have sometimes felt alone as I've tried to navigate the challenges of parenting and make decisions about the future. Just last week, I met with my financial planner to adjust the college savings plan I am pursuing for my son. I so wished I could call Dad to talk through the options. But I prayed about it, and slept on it, and when I woke the next morning, I had made a decision and felt at peace. God, you are there. Please help me to remember this, and that my strength to face life's trials comes from you.

Fear thou not; for I am with thee: be not dismayed;
for I am thy God: I will strengthen thee; yea,
I will help thee; yea, I will uphold thee
with the right hand of my righteousness.

—Isaiah 41:10

As a cop, I am used to handling trouble. I like to think of myself as pretty unflappable, and my family and friends look to me when they are uncertain or afraid. But last week, my teenage son was involved in an auto accident, and when I got the call, it was still unclear as to whether there were any fatalities. I was filled with fear as my wife and I drove as fast as we could to the hospital. What if our son didn't make it? What if he lived but had sustained brain damage? My wife and I held hands as we sped through the night streets, and began to pray out loud. God, you were there with us, in our car; you got us to the hospital emergency room safely; you were there when the doctor greeted us with news that our son's legs had been shattered in the accident, but that he will live. Our boy's road to recovery is going to be a long one. We still don't know if he will ever walk again without aid. It is a hard time for our family, but God, you have always been there for us. Whatever lies ahead, we will not make this journey alone. Please help me to remember, on days when I falter, that your strength is the ultimate antidote to fear and stress.

Be strong and of a good courage, fear not,
nor be afraid of them: for the Lord thy God,
he it is that doth go with thee;
he will not fail thee, nor forsake thee.

—Deuteronomy 31:6

God, there are times when we must be brave and face an adversary. I work at an ad agency and we are currently bidding on some client work. I'll be making a presentation and competing against rival firms for a lucrative account. Sometimes the competition can get cutthroat. The main challenger has a reputation for badmouthing the competition, and I'm not looking forward to interacting with this gentleman the day of the presentations. God, please strengthen me so that I might face my rival with grace.

The Lord will give strength unto his people; the Lord will bless his people with peace.

—Psalm 29:11

God strengthens individuals, but he also strengthens groups. This thought gave me comfort last night as I prepared for a summer mission trip. I will be traveling to Oklahoma to help rebuild homes destroyed in a tornado, and have been charged with directing eight college-aged kids from my church. I am a skilled carpenter but less certain about leading a group. God, I pray you will grant my team the strength and cohesiveness we need to do our jobs well.

Lord, thank you for calling me to yourself and then giving me your Spirit to strengthen me—heart, soul, mind, and body—to work in ways that bring honor to you. This goal of being a model of good works in every respect makes me realize how much I need you each moment. And as I grow in a life of doing what is right and true and good, help me grow in humility as well, remembering that you are the source of my strength.

Lord, please be my strength. When I am scared, please make me brave. When I am unsteady, please bring your stability to me. I look to your power for an escape from the pain. I welcome your comfort.

In the aftermath of tragedy, it takes energy and courage to rebuild, Great Architect. How amazing that your gift of courage translates worry into energy and fear into determination. Help us recognize ill feelings as potential fuel that can be turned into reconstruction tools. Through your grace, we've courageously faced what was our lives and we are now off to see what our lives can be.

Jesus saith unto him, Rise, take up thy bed, and walk.

—John 5:8

Sometimes I am afraid. Sometimes the path before me seems almost impossible. Last year, I decided to return to school. The office where I work indicated that I would have a better chance of advancing if I pursued a graduate degree. But I was anxious. School has never come easily to me, and at this stage of my life, I have myriad responsibilities, including a house and two active children under the age of five. But I prayed about it, and worked with my wife to figure out a humane course schedule that makes sense for our family. Though it will take a long time, I will eventually earn my degree. This first year I have been gratified to learn that I can keep up with my coursework and still make time for my job and family. It isn't always easy, though, and I pray for strength every day. I have learned that if I have faith, God will help me take on enormous challenges.

Father God, when I'm tempted to give up on a task, it helps to read about Abraham, Moses, Joseph, David, Job—all those whose times of trial and perseverance are so beautifully preserved for us through your Word. Once we are attuned to your plan for our lives, we can continue with the certainty that you always complete what you start. We can stand firmly on your promises, confident that you will give us the strength we need to keep going. Thank you for the faith of the ages, Lord! It is also the faith for today.

Be strong and of a good courage; be not afraid, neither be thou dismayed: for the Lord thy God is with thee whithersoever thou goest.

—Joshua 1:9

Thank you, Lord, that you're never missing in action—that you're with me all the time, everywhere, without fail. Please keep this knowledge in the forefront of my mind today so I'll be encouraged and emboldened to move through each challenge without feeling intimidated, fearful, or ashamed. May I always be kept safe because of your keeping power at work in my life. In your name, I pray.

Some days the race feels like a sprint, Lord, and on other days, a marathon. On the harder days, please infuse my spirit with your strength and steadfastness. I want to run and finish well. Thank you for promising not to stop working until my faith is complete.

Spirit, help me live one day at a time so that I may meet each day's challenges with grace, courage, and hope. Shelter me from the fears of the future and the anguish of the past. Keep my mind and heart focused on the present, where the true gift of happiness and healing is to be found.

Compassion

And when she had opened it, she saw the child:
and, behold, the babe wept.
And she had compassion on him, and said,
This is one of the Hebrews' children.

—Exodus 2:6

My wife and I, unable to bear a child of our own, have recently begun thinking about adoption. The thought of helping a parentless child is meaningful to us, and we've started investigating what it might mean to adopt a child from another culture. Our friends recently adopted a little girl from China, and their journey and the joy they've experienced fill us with hope. We know we have a lot of love to give. And how expanding our little family would enrich our lives! God, please guide us as we endeavor to reach out to a child in need. Please keep us humble and cognizant of how much we stand to gain by showing compassion to another.

And Saul said, Blessed be ye of the Lord;
for ye have compassion on me.

—1 Samuel 23:21

My kindergarten-age daughter has had a "best friend" since preschool, but recently the other little girl has been unkind to my daughter, pointedly excluding her at recess and talking about her unkindly to the other girls in their class. After more than a month of this behavior, my wife spoke to the other girl's mother, and the woman was defensive, even hostile, intimating that it was our daughter's fault and that she was provoking her child in some way. My wife gently persisted, and as we talked to the other family and our own child, it became apparent that the other little girl is jealous of our daughter's reading ability. Though it helped to understand the situation, matters haven't changed much between the girls. We have alerted the teacher to the situation, and encouraged our daughter to seek other playmates. She's made the adjustment, but my wife and I were disappointed at the hostility the other mother showed us, and her unwillingness to hold her own daughter accountable. Dear Lord, help me to feel (and demonstrate) compassion for this family, even if they do not respond in kind, and even as I am an advocate for my child. Please help me to proceed with grace.

Watch, dear Lord, with those who wake,
or watch, or weep tonight,
and give your angels charge over those who sleep.
Tend your sick ones, O Lord Christ,
Rest your weary ones.
Bless your dying ones.
Soothe your suffering ones.
Pity your afflicted ones.
Shield your joyous ones.
And all for your love's sake.
Amen.

—St. Augustine

But thou, O Lord, art a God full of compassion,
and gracious, long suffering,
and plenteous in mercy and truth.

—Psalm 86:15

It is easy to be judgmental. It is easy to write another person off when they fall short of our expectations. Even those we love will disappoint us. Yesterday I was short with my sister when she called to let me know that she won't be able to take our mother shopping this weekend. I was counting on her help, and at first, I wouldn't let myself hear her explanation—her own daughter is sick, and her husband, my brother-in-law, has been pulling extra shifts at work. It took effort for me to overcome my own annoyance and listen to what she had to say. Dear Lord, help me to remember that compassion comes from you. May I be inspired by the compassion you show me every day, and may I in turn show compassion to others.

Then the lord of that servant was moved
with compassion, and loosed him,
and forgave him the debt.

—Matthew 18:27

God, I aspire to be the person you want me to be, to live the life you want for me, but sometimes I struggle. I have a friend to whom I lent money; it has become apparent that not only will he not be able to repay what he owes, but he has also been avoiding me. I caught sight of him in town yesterday, and he literally crossed the street to avoid any interaction. Even when I called out to him, he would not meet my eye. I know he is ashamed that he cannot repay me, but I'm disappointed in him. I wish I'd never lent him the money. Please grant me the compassion and grace to forgive this debt, and move on.

Therefore his sisters sent unto him, saying, Lord, behold, he whom thou lovest is sick.

—John 11:3

I move through my days with a sense of purpose, but sometimes I am so consumed by the immediate to-dos that I forget to be open to—or even aware of—opportunities for compassion. This week was no exception. My mind has been on a tight work deadline, and at night, I've been tackling a series of home repairs. It was only when my wife sat me down and made me put my phone aside that I slowed down long enough for her to share that a close friend of ours has been battling depression. If I'd been paying attention, I might have seen the signals. This friend is usually good about staying in touch, but I hadn't heard from him in several months. "Why don't you give him a call?" was my wife's gentle suggestion. God, help me to be sensitive to those I love, and those in need. Jesus was responsive when he learned that Lazarus was sick; may I likewise show compassion.

The day was long, the burden I had borne
Seemed heavier that I could no longer bear;
And then it lifted—but I did not know
Someone had knelt in prayer.
Had taken me to God that very hour,
And asked the easing of the load, and He
In infinite compassion, had stooped down
And lifted the burden from me.
We cannot tell how often as we pray
For some bewildered one, hurt and distressed,
The answer comes, but many times these hearts
Find sudden peace and rest.
Someone had prayed, and faith, a lifted hand
Reached up to God, and He reached down that day.
So many, many hearts have need of prayer—
Then, let us, let us pray.

—Author Unknown

Gratitude

This is the day which the Lord hath made;
we will rejoice and be glad in it.

—Psalm 118:24

Earlier this week I took it upon myself to visit a local botanic garden. It is just minutes from my home, but I don't often think to go there. I went on a weekday this time, which meant that the park was much less crowded. I appreciated the solitude, and chose to walk a path that winds around a small lake and through pinewoods. The path is made of wood chips, and as I rounded a bend, I heard a crunching noise, as if someone else were walking and enjoying the bright day. I expected to encounter another hiker. Imagine my surprise when I instead found myself face to face with a deer! The doe looked at me with clear brown eyes, unafraid, and I tried to remain perfectly still. I do not think I exaggerate when I say that we shared a moment; then she regained herself and bounded away. I am so glad I made the effort to visit the botanic garden that day! Dear Lord, thank you for an encounter that filled my spirit. Thank you for this world.

In every thing give thanks: for this is the will of God in Christ Jesus concerning you.

—1 Thessalonians 5:18

It's been a challenging year. I work in a volatile industry, and was laid off after my company merged with another. The layoff came as a surprise, and at a time when my wife and I have been hit with some unexpected expenses, chiefly for home maintenance as we deal with an old roof and an older furnace. And yet, there are blessings. My company gave me a generous severance, which allows me time to figure out next steps for my career without panicking. We have savings that will help us finance the new roof, and I am reminded to be grateful that we have a roof over our heads! Ours is a happy home, filled with children and pets, books and music and sunlight. Dear Lord, even in hard times, there is always something for which I can be grateful.

And whatsoever ye do in word or deed,
do all in the name of the Lord Jesus,
giving thanks to God and the Father by him.

—Colossians 3:17

Some days are joyful. Yesterday was such a day. I attended church, it was a good sermon, and as the pastor led us in prayer, my thankfulness sprang forth easily. It felt good to thank you, God. When I walked out into the world, it was as though I was smiling and the world smiled back at me. At lunch I swapped jokes with our waitress and thanked her by leaving a good tip.

When we stopped by the nursing home where my dad lives, I appreciated the time I was able to spend laughing and talking with some of the residents. One older gentleman who served in World War II relayed a story about his experiences, and I thanked him for sharing. "You are a happy person," he commented. "I can tell by your gratitude." I was deeply touched by his statement, and reminded that showing appreciation to others, not only in words but in actions, is one way of passing on the thankfulness we feel in our own hearts. Dear Lord, help me to always give thanks to you in the way I conduct myself.

Lord, if only everyone could adopt your law of love as our neighbors have. I thank you for sending good friends who are always ready to provide our children with shelter and a cookie in any emergency, to lend equipment or advice, to offer an occasional ride or a meal—to help out in any way they can. Where would we be without their valued assistance? I am grateful for their kindness, their willingness, and their generous spirits. Bless these loving people, Father, who are your hands reaching out to care for us. Please make me a good neighbor to them, and may I find many opportunities to return your love by helping them when they are in need.

Wherefore we receiving a kingdom
which cannot be moved, let us have grace,
whereby we may serve God acceptably
with reverence and godly fear.

—Hebrews 12:28

I attend church regularly, but I find that the place I feel closest to God is in nature. My home backs up to a forest preserve, and whenever I can, I try to hike the trails there. As I walk through these trees, which existed before I was born and will stand tall long after my death, I am reminded of God's permanence. I am at an age when some of my friends are facing real limitations due to health issues, and slowly they are passing away. But being in the woods lifts my heart as I am surrounded by leafy evidence that God's presence is everlasting. During my walks, I have my best conversations with God. I talk to him about how grateful I am for the life he has given me and that I am still healthy enough to hike, fast and for great distance. I am also grateful that when my time on Earth is finally done, I will move on to a place where I will abide permanently in God's grace and love. God's natural creation is but a taste of what is to come. Lord, thank you for recognizing the gratitude that underlies my simple and perhaps unconventional worship in the woods.

Thanksgiving is nothing if not a glad and reverent lifting of the heart to God in honour and praise for His goodness.

—James R. Miller

Glorious indeed is the world of God around us, but more glorious the world of God within us.

—Henry Wadsworth Longfellow

O give thanks unto the Lord; for he is good:
for his mercy endureth for ever.

—Psalm 136:1

My son Tad is three, and he can be sweet one moment, then overcome by storms of temper the next. The other day, he was tired and had a meltdown when I asked him to put away his toys before dinner. As a parent, I am not always as even-tempered as I should be. But this was one of those times when I had the patience to do it right. I drew Tad onto my lap and rocked him until he calmed down. As my son and I sat together, looking out at the quiet evening street, I thought of God's patience when I rail against the storms of life. Lord, I am grateful to you because you are always good and merciful to me.

For all the things we have to be grateful for in this life, one of the most encouraging for us as children of God is that the best is yet to come. Our time here is just a warm-up for what lies ahead. Everything on the earth that is marked by decay, decline, disease, and death will no longer exist in heaven. God will bring Christ's victory to fullness when he does away with the old and ushers us into the new. Give thanks with all your heart today, for no matter what your pain, loss, failure, or fear might be, in Christ you have victory over it and a glorious future beyond it!

Dear Lord, grant that I may keep an eternal perspective from which I can thank you for the best that is yet to come.

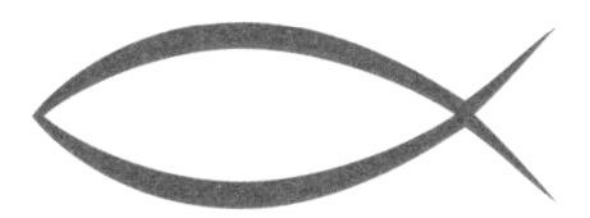

Gateway to Thanks

Open to me the gates of righteousness:
I will go into them, and I will praise the Lord.

—Psalm 118:19

It's interesting to note that when we are not walking in the ways of God, we are unwilling (or perhaps unable) to give him proper thanks. When we're doing our own thing, we tend to grumble and groan our way through the day rather than thank and praise our God. When we purpose to walk in God's ways and listen to his voice, however, we get so full of gratitude and joy that thanksgiving becomes second nature. If we've wandered away from the gate of righteousness that leads to thanksgiving, let's stop this very second and turn back. The gate is before us now—it's time to enter in.

Lord, free my heart from things that would lead me away from the gate of righteousness. May I enter through that gate today and give you thanks because you alone are my salvation.

Let the people praise thee, O God; let all the people praise thee. O let the nations be glad and sing for joy: for thou shalt judge the people righteously, and govern the nations upon earth.

—Psalm 67:3–4

There isn't a person on this earth God doesn't want to see enter into the joy and blessing of his kingdom. What is your heritage, your nationality, your culture, your race? God loves you, and he loves your people! He welcomes your praise and the praises of your people. He longs to bless you, and he longs to bless your people. Come worship him today, for your God is a God for all peoples, and that includes you!

All of us have come from you, O Lord. You have made the peoples of the earth, and we belong to you. May I praise you with all the peoples of God today, for you have welcomed us freely into your kingdom.

Marriage

And the Lord God said, It is not good
that the man should be alone;
I will make him an help meet for him.

—Genesis 2:18

My wife and I have been married for 25 years. Around the time we celebrated that milestone anniversary, we each began to pursue self-employment ventures that allow us to work from home. Several friends have laughingly asked if we get on one another's nerves, but working from home has actually been a real joy for us both. We like working together in the living room with music playing in the background. We both love the company of our cats. I really enjoy that my wife and I can eat lunch together, and sometimes we'll take a break in the afternoon and swim laps at the Y. My wife is my best friend. God, thank you for the everyday companionship that a strong marriage brings.

And above all things have fervent charity among yourselves: for charity shall cover the multitude of sins.

—1 Peter 4:8

My wife and I are newly married, and we have encountered some growing pains as we adjust to sharing a home and making a life together. One persistent source of discord is the fact that I am something of a neatnik, while my wife is more relaxed about keeping our apartment tidy. I can see that she tries, but it still drives me a little crazy when she leaves dirty dishes on the counter, or toothpaste spatters in the sink. These are such little things, but sometimes they get to me, and I said as much to my father the last time we were together. Dad has been married to my mom for more than 30 years, and he responded to me with gentle humor: "Choose your battles, son, and remember: love helps us overlook one another's flaws." My parents have an extraordinarily loving marriage, and Dad's words have stayed with me. Dear Lord, please help me remember that love is the root of a strong marriage, and that love helps us accept our partners as they are, warts and all.

Lord, we lift up our marriage to you with thanks for the gift you gave us when you first brought us together: it isn't as fresh and new as it was when you created it for us, Lord, so we ask your blessing again. Wrap the life we share in your protective arms so that the world will never be able to tear us apart. Fill us anew with the precious love you gave us for one another. Hold us firmly in your eternal love. Amen.

Marriage, Lord, is like a garden. You don't keep digging up a plant to see if its roots are growing. Sustain us, for there are seasons of fading flowers just as there are seasons of blossom and fruit. While ripening to become useful, may we love one another with the same trust and patience you, gardener of the world, show toward us.

And if one prevail against him,
two shall withstand him; and a threefold cord
is not quickly broken.

—Ecclesiastes 4:12

My wife and I don't attend church every Sunday, but each weekend we make time to read scripture and talk about the week, which we try to view through the lens of spirituality. A difficult coworker, good news in our extended families—we'll discuss the good and the bad and talk about how God informs each ebb and flow. Sometimes we'll share a joy, such as the time my wife built a new bird feeder and we both discovered the great calm and pleasure we derived from watching the sparrows and finches. I think we both gain a lot from these quiet, regular moments of sharing. The Bible reminds me how your presence in my life, and my wife's life, creates a powerful "threefold cord." God, if my marriage is grounded in you, it will always be strong.

With all lowliness and meekness, with longsuffering, forbearing one another in love; Endeavouring to keep the unity of the Spirit in the bond of peace.

—Ephesians 4:2–3

One of many things I like about my wife is her ability to laugh at herself. She doesn't take herself too seriously, and because I admire that quality in her, and know that I myself can tend to pride, I try as best I can to emulate her humility. Just yesterday, we were talking about my efforts to fix the sink in the bathroom, and when I caught myself becoming defensive (even, I have to admit, a little self-important), I tried to turn things around by joking. I think my wife was probably relieved to see me making an effort, and so she took up with the joke. Within moments we were both laughing. Things could have gone one way but they took a better turn. Dear Lord, thank you for helping me to remember the importance of humility in a marriage.

What therefore God hath joined together,
let not man put asunder.

—Mark 10:9

My wife and I have encountered a rough patch in our marriage. Our youngest child recently began college, and transitioning to an "empty nest" home has been harder on us both than we anticipated. My wife, who misses our sons, has started a new job. She's not home as much just as I've begun contemplating taking early retirement. So many days we seem to be at cross-purposes—we seem to want different things! But this morning when we sat down together over coffee, my wife reminded me that over the years, we have weathered many storms in our marriage—job loss, the deaths of our parents, our middle son's struggles with schoolwork and drugs. Each time we have prevailed together. It was a good conversation, and I think we felt closer to one another than we have in months. Dear Lord, you have joined my wife and me. You have blessed our partnership. To succeed, we must take the long view!

Almighty God, I honestly don't know how a marriage survives without forgiveness. In fact, maybe the marriages without it don't survive. Thank you for a forgiving wife, Lord. Because she forgives me so often, it's much easier for me to forgive her when she does something thoughtless. Forgiveness prevents the weeds from taking root in a relationship and provides an environment where love can grow. Bless our marriage, Lord, and keep it well watered with forgiveness.

Lord, how grateful I am to have found the love of my life. May I never take her for granted. May I focus on her strengths and be quick to forget any silly disagreement. Help me to be her encourager and her friend. Protect the bond between us, Lord. Keep it strong, healthy, and loving.

My heart is full of gratitude, O God, when I think of my wife and the miraculous way you brought us together. I realize now it was you who chose her to be the mother of my children.

She is a woman of integrity and worth, generous and loving, with the ability to laugh at herself—a perfect combination for a parent.

Her loyalty and faithfulness are unquestioned. I am proud to be her husband and prouder still to have my children call her Mom. I humbly thank you, Lord, for this uncommon blessing: You have given to our children and me a faithful woman and a woman of faith.

Pride

Let nothing be done through strife or vainglory; but in lowliness of mind let each esteem other better than themselves.

—Philippians 2:3

I was proud when my middle-school-aged son participated in a local speech competition this spring. He placed well in the district levels, and will be moving on to compete at the county level. The county level, of course, will feature winners from other districts. All these kids will be "cream of the crop," which means that the competition will be stiffer. The event takes place next week, and my son is a little nervous about how well he will place. What if he does not get as high a ranking at the county level as he did at the district level? My wife and I have counseled him to just try hard, enjoy himself, and never lose sight of the difference between healthy competition and destructive rivalry. Dear Lord, thank you for guiding my son and his peers to respect one another as they strive to do their best.

Charity suffereth long, and is kind; charity envieth not; charity vaunteth not itself, is not puffed up.

—1 Corinthians 13:4

Sometimes pride gets the better of me. When things are going well in my life, I am not above indulging in a certain prideful righteousness. Last week at work, I learned I'd earned a significant bonus for my quarterly sales. My first thought was, "Well, I deserve it! I worked harder than anyone else." In fact, I was almost smug. I felt certain that I'd bested Glenn, my coworker; he and I are "friendly rivals" when it comes to sales numbers. But too much pride can be much like eating too much dessert—it might feel good at first, but it can catch up to a person. As the day wore on, I was, I'll confess, almost sick of myself—a little self-congratulation goes a long way, it turns out. I decided to take a walk to clear my head. The neighborhood where I work has some interesting restaurants and shops. I passed a cool new donut shop known for its interesting flavor combinations. Out of curiosity, I stopped to look in. Suddenly remembering God's exhortation to combat pride with charity, I ordered a couple dozen pastries and brought them back to the office. When I arrived bearing that bright pink box, my coworkers were happy, and I felt good. God, thank you for reminding me to look outside myself.

He that is void of wisdom despiseth his neighbour: but a man of understanding holdeth his peace.

—Proverbs 11:12

I am proud of my daughter. At 13, she is wise beyond her years. She is well liked by her teachers and peers, and a gifted musician. It's tempting, sometimes, to want to broadcast her accomplishments—the straight As she got on her last report card; the fact that she snagged a lead in the spring play. But I remember my mom used to shake her head when she'd encounter acquaintances who always seemed to go on and on about their own kids. She'd say to me privately, "Your dad and I are so proud of you kids, but our children speak for themselves by the way they are in the world." I was always struck by her grace, and the faith she had in us kids. Her example is an inspiration to me now that I am a parent myself. Dear Lord, may I steer clear of bragging; rather may I celebrate the joy I take in my daughter with quiet grace.

Lord, my pride sometimes tempts me to judge others. From reality TV to social networking, it seems that very little in life is private anymore. This does not explain away some of the comments I find myself making, though. Throughout your Word, you make it clear that your gift of salvation is available to everyone. Put this utmost in my mind when my pride tempts me to pass judgment on those around me.

Lord, it is tempting and easy to cast a scornful eye on those around us and note every fault. When my pride tempts me to do so, prompt me to turn the magnifying glass on myself instead. If I keep in mind how much I need your forgiveness every day, my love for you will never grow cold. I know you are willing to forgive each and every fault if I only ask.

Pride goeth before destruction,
and an haughty spirit before a fall.

—Proverbs 16:18

It used to be important to me to have the largest house on the block. It used to matter what type of car I drove. I took pride in my professional accomplishments, and I treated our possessions like personal trophies. I even began to pray less and stop reading the Bible as I focused on activities that would enrich my career and bring gains that are more material. Then, last year, we discovered that my wife is seriously ill. We were blindsided by the news; I had thought, on some level, that we were impervious to disaster. I thought my worldly success, which brought material riches, kept us safe. In these last months, as my wife has endured chemotherapy and bravely battled cancer, I have been humbled. I have also found solace in my faith. God, too much pride in myself made me blind to what truly matters. Thank you for being there for me and those I love.

Father, it stings when the ones I love correct me. I don't like to be wrong or feel like I'm being criticized. But that's just wounded pride revealing itself. Deep down I appreciate learning the truth so I can learn and grow. Flattery feels nice in the moment, but it doesn't do much real good. People who risk hurting me because they love me are the ones I should listen to. Help me get over my wounded pride quickly and move on in light of what I've learned. And bless those who care enough for me to speak the truth in love.

I have therefore whereof I may glory through Jesus Christ in those things which pertain to God.

—Romans 15:17

Yesterday I took my son Jason and a few of his friends to pack food for a local religious organization that helps feed families in need. The kids were happy and excited. The warehouse where we worked had music playing, and our group felt good about the amount of work we got done. That night, as I tucked my son into bed, I told him that I was very proud of what he'd accomplished. "We did a good thing, didn't we?" he said. We talked about the kids who will benefit from the food; we talked about how doing good is one way to honor God. Then Jason asked if it was okay to be proud of the work we'd done that day. "Sometimes pride is bad, right?" he said. I agreed that sometimes it is. Sometimes pride can hobble us, or make us blind to things that are more important. "But it's totally okay to be proud of our works for God!" I assured him. "Helping makes me feel good," Jason agreed soberly. I hugged him, and felt so close to my boy. God, thank you for the opportunity to do good in your name.

Gracious God, being a father is the most important calling of my life, but I confess that it has been difficult to keep going at such an exhausting pace. Pride has kept me from asking for more help fulfilling all of my children's needs.

Lord, break down this barrier of pride within me, and make me humble enough to admit to others that I need help. My wife, parents, and friends are capable of sharing the load, if only I will let them.

Help me to convince myself that I need a break once in a while, that I am not being selfish when I take one, and that a relaxed dad can be a more loving dad.

Self-Improvement

I can do all things through Christ
which strengtheneth me.

—Philippians 4:13

I have always been a social drinker. Shy by nature, having a beer helps me relax and feel more comfortable in social settings. But lately I've noticed that I've begun to rely on a drink to unwind after work, or to gear up for a stressful encounter. When I made the decision to cut back, I was surprised and dismayed to discover how dependent I've become on alcohol to fill an emotional need. I think the best path for me is abstinence. Now that I no longer can rely on alcohol to "take off the edge," each day is a struggle. Lord, please give me the strength to persevere in eschewing alcohol. I know my health and well-being will benefit. I thank you for your grace.

Let your light so shine before men,
that they may see your good works,
and glorify your Father which is in heaven.

—Matthew 5:16

I am by nature a quiet and reserved person; like my parents before me, I've always believed actions speak louder than words. When our pastor recently gave a sermon challenging the congregation to go out and share with others the way God has helped us grow, I initially felt resistant. "Not my style!" was my knee-jerk reaction. And yet talking with the pastor after the service, I realized that showing reverence to God could take different forms. I don't have to go out and preach about how God has helped me improve myself. I can simply demonstrate growth through my actions, whether I'm quitting smoking or getting better at managing my temper. If people ask, as someone recently did, "How did you quit smoking?" I can always give a simple answer: "Prayer." Lord, I can demonstrate my beliefs and inspire others by always striving to better myself. Please help me to honor you in this way.

Thy word is a lamp unto my feet,
and a light unto my path.

—Psalm 119:105

As a college student living in the United States, I have many advantages, and it's easy to fall into the trap of feeling that, given all I have going for me, I should "be the best at everything." I am hard on myself when I don't get the best grade, for example, or when I perceive that I'm not as physically fit as some of my dorm mates. God, help me to remember that there is always room for improvement, a condition I share with everyone else on Earth, and that your Word can comfort me, guide me, and serve as the ultimate "self-improvement manual."

The Lord is not slack concerning his promise,
as some men count slackness;
but is longsuffering to us-ward,
not willing that any should perish,
but that all should come to repentance.

—2 Peter 3:9

My mom, a physical therapist, sometimes says, "Two steps forward, one step back," to clients who feel discouraged about the long road to recovery. "But you'll get there," she always adds. Mom is a spiritual person, and she shared with me once that not only does she think her maxim applies to any process of self-improvement, it reminds her of God's faith in us. I was deeply struck by her observation! Self-improvement is a long haul, marked by setbacks and detours. And yet, God, you always are patient with me, and believe that I can better myself. Thank you for believing in my potential and efforts; I am bolstered by your patience and love.

Lord, make me an instrument of your peace;
where there is hatred, let me sow love;
where there is injury, pardon;
where there is doubt, faith;
where there is despair, hope;
where there is darkness, light;
and where there is sadness, joy.
Divine Master, grant that I may not so much seek
to be consoled as to console;
to be understood as to understand;
to be loved as to love.
For it is in giving that we receive,
it is in pardoning that we are pardoned,
and it is in dying that we are born to eternal life.

—St. Francis of Assisi

Therefore if any man be in Christ,
he is a new creature: old things are passed away;
behold, all things are become new.

—2 Corinthians 5:17

When I was a boy, my favorite uncle used to take me fishing on summer evenings when he was in town. Uncle Will was a truck driver, a job that frequently took him away from his family and friends for days at a time, and he formed some bad habits eating alone on the road. Perhaps not surprisingly, after a number of years of this, my uncle developed diabetes and high blood pressure. Will's doctor warned that his eating habits were going to kill him—a serious wake-up call that prompted some life changes. I still remember the evening my uncle and I were out on the river, hoping to catch a pike but mostly reeling in bluegills. He told me it was through God's grace that he was able to change his ways. "I'm healthier," Uncle Will said when I complimented his weight loss. And then he added something I've never forgotten: "God didn't just help me get better, he transformed me. Not just on the outside. On the inside." Lord, you are there to help us better ourselves, not just externally, but internally. Thank you for being there.

It's agonizingly hard to "come clean" when one bad choice has led to another and has snowballed out of control . . . when it's time to ask for help, confess folly, swallow pride, and reveal the mess. But we have a merciful God. We have a God who does not chide those who turn to him with a sincere heart of repentance. No matter how far down the road of self-sufficiency we've wandered, he's just behind us, ready to embrace us if we'll just turn around and ask him to lead us back in the right direction.

Merciful Lord, when my self-sufficient ways lead me into trouble, help me turn around quickly to find your mercy and your way.

Try to maintain your Christian profession among your comrades. I need not caution you against strong drink as useless and hurtful, nor against profanity, so common among soldiers. Both these practices you abhor. Aim to take at once a decided stand for God. If practicable have prayers regularly in your tent, or unite with fellow-disciples in prayer meetings in the camp. Should preaching be accessible, always be a hearer. Let the world know that you are a Christian. Read a chapter in the New Testament, which your mother gave you, every morning and evening, when you can, and engage in secret prayer to God for his Holy Spirit to guide and sustain you. I would rather hear of your death than of the shipwreck of your faith and good conscience.

—Excerpt from "Soldier Life" (1882) by Carlton McCarthy

Work and Leadership

Come unto me, all ye that labour and are heavy laden, and I will give you rest.

—Matthew 11:28

I run my own business, and while I appreciate the many perks of my lifestyle—working from home, a flexible schedule, being my own boss—I sometimes find myself burning the midnight oil and working too hard in an effort to "keep up." The other night I found myself awake, crunching numbers, well into the early hours of the morning. Those dark hours can be lonely ones. As I wrapped up for the night and put my calculator aside, I felt worn out—not just physically, but emotionally. But as I made my way up the stairs to bed, I thought about Christ's promise of giving rest to the weary, and I was comforted. "I'm too tired to do anything more," I thought and, giving over the day's work to Jesus, slept well. God, thank you for the gift of your son, who is there for us to share our burden and restore us with rest.

And Moses said unto God, Who am I,
that I should go unto Pharaoh,
and that I should bring forth the children
of Israel out of Egypt?

—Exodus 3:11

My uncle, the president of a paper company, used to paraphrase Shakespeare and say, "Heavy is the head that wears the crown." I was a child at the time and didn't really understand what he was talking about. Now that I am an adult and hold a leadership position at work, I think I have an idea of what Shakespeare and my uncle might had been saying. I have many employees looking to me for guidance, advice, and a secure livelihood. Sometimes, when we are dealing with difficult clients or getting pressure from our shareholders, I question whether I am fit to lead. I must remind myself: even Moses had doubts, and God strengthens us. Dear Lord, thank you for giving me the grit and wisdom to effectively direct those who look to me for leadership.

Let him that stole steal no more:
but rather let him labour,
working with his hands the thing which is good,
that he may have to give to him that needeth.

—Ephesians 4:28

My 14-year-old son Cal began high school this year. He's always run with a nice group of kids, but this year he drifted into a new crowd and my wife and I were dismayed to see some changes in his behavior. He stopped taking his schoolwork seriously and his grades dropped. Cal's attitude at home became blasé and sullen. It seemed to be "cool" to not care about school or his family. Worried about the threat of drugs and alcohol, my wife and I tried various things, from grounding our son and withdrawing privileges to encouraging him to join a club at school. But it was only when my dad introduced Cal to woodworking that we saw some of the old Cal return. Working creatively with his hands seems almost therapeutic for our son. He likes going over to my dad's workshop. He likes creating something that lasts. Cal hasn't been hanging out as much with the new group of friends. He's working on a series of bookshelves for his room. God, thank you for helping us to help Cal. Finding constructive things to do is a great way to re-channel energy that's been misspent.

Answering the Call

Work is good right now, God of all labor, and I think I know why: You and I are working together. Is this what it is to be called?

I think it must be, for you are the source of my talents, for which I am grateful. Through the support of others, gifted teachers, mentors, and leaders, and through those willing to take a chance on me despite the odds, you have always been present, and I am grateful for that, too.

Although this sense that I am doing what you intend for me is usually just a delicious, split-second awareness, O God, it's enough to keep me going when I'm tired, frustrated, and unclear about my next step. Our companionship of call to vocation is not an instant process, but rather a shared journey. Keep me listening, watching.

I am glad we share this working venture, for on the job and off, I am blessed.

And whatsoever ye do, do it heartily,
as to the Lord, and not unto men.

—Colossians 3:23

I have always liked the expression, "You aren't the boss of me!" I'm an independent person, I run my own business, and I like being in control. And yet, sometimes I need to be reminded that there is someone I'm answerable to, and that someone is God. God asks that I be accountable in my actions, in the choices I make, and in the example I set for others—at home and in the world. I try to live my life with abandon, and when I keep God's Word first and foremost in my thinking, I find I can live fully in a way that feels good. God, you are my ultimate boss and I thank you!

For which of you, intending to build a tower, sitteth not down first, and counteth the cost, whether he have sufficient to finish it?

—Luke 14:28

My wife Meg and I recently bought our first house, a little brick bungalow with beautiful bay windows. We've lived in apartments up until now, and suddenly we are homeowners, with all that entails: a postage-stamp-sized yard, a room we can use as an office, and even a guest room. It's been exciting to transform the little bungalow from a house into our home, and we've spent time and money in our efforts to do so. There are the practical purchases, like a small lawn mower, and then there are what Meg and I call "fun" purchases, like new curtains for the living room. There are many more things we'd like to do—the current light fixture in the dining room is pretty ugly, for instance, and we'd like to replace it—but we work hard for our income, and know we need to pace ourselves financially. As Meg reminded me the other day, God instructs us to plan carefully down to the last detail, and calculate the costs of everything we do. The new light fixture is going to have to wait, but in the meantime, we are wise to be happy with the fruits of our labors—the blessing of a new home.

Lord, we pray for all those in positions of leadership in our government. The pressures and influences on them are of a magnitude we can only imagine. Watch over them, Lord. Reach out to them with your grace, and instill in them your character, your priorities, and your vision for our country and our world.

Great leaders may be born and not made. But they can only be elected if good people vote for them.

For the Boss

Be the leader you were meant to be today.

Find courage to temper your business goals with an eye toward human compassion.

Carefully weigh the consequences of every tough decision you make—the effects on the company and the impact on all who work within it.

Know that one greater than you goes before you and stands behind you, offering great wisdom.

And in this knowledge, seek to lead just as he did—being servant of all.

Forgiveness

And forgive us our debts,
as we forgive our debtors.

—Matthew 6:12

In quarrels with family members or friends, I am usually quick to forgive and move on. Life is too short for grudges! And yet, one area in which forgiveness does not come so easily for me is a pardon of debt. I recently loaned money to a friend, and he has been almost cavalier about paying me back. Though we agreed he would repay me in full by last week, he has not done so. I am surprised at how much the situation bothers me, but it was a considerable sum. I see my friend at work, and these last few days, though he seems unconcerned, I have found myself struggling to stay positive and gracious when we are together. It's uncomfortable to bring up, but I know I must talk with him about the loan. God, please grant me the serenity and wisdom to approach this sensitive matter with grace. Teach me how to forgive my friend if he cannot repay me as quickly or completely as I might have hoped.

I wish I had your ability to forget sin, Lord. How marvelous that you promise to remove our sin as far as the east is from the west and to remember it no more! I'm just not good at forgetting sins, even if I can forgive them. It's my nature to hold onto grudges and to remember everything from the unintentional slight to the egregious sin. Help me, Lord. Give me your amazing ability to forgive—and forget.

Thank you for your forgiveness that forgets as well, my Lord. Help me to learn to forgive others and myself that way too.

And when ye stand praying, forgive,
if ye have ought against any:
that your Father also which is in heaven
may forgive you your trespasses.

—Mark 11:25

When my dear wife died of cancer, many friends stepped forward, but some—even friends I hold dear—disappointed me by not being there for me as much as I might have hoped. Death is a frightening thing. My wife's death was untimely, and I tried to remember that people's lives are complex. Sometimes, I imagine, my expectations were simply too high. And yet it was painful for me to understand that some loved ones could not, for whatever reason, be there for me in my grief. It was only through prayer that I gained a measure of relief, perspective, and calm. God, thank you for always being there to listen to me. Prayer puts me in the right frame of mind to forgive others and, sometimes, to forgive myself.

Lord, I know I need to forgive someone who wronged me. The problem is, I can't honestly say I want to forgive her. For some reason I enjoy telling myself that I was right and she was wrong. Convict me, Lord! Don't let me allow this thing to fester any longer for my own selfish satisfaction. Give me your strength to forgive so that I can put this behind me, and behind her, too. Restore our relationship in the light of forgiveness. Amen.

To err is human, to forgive divine.

—Alexander Pope

In whom we have redemption through his blood,
the forgiveness of sins,
according to the riches of his grace.

—Ephesians 1:7

Some days are better than others. Yesterday I was patient when my son forgot his books at school (again), when a coworker slighted me, and when I got the wrong change at the movie theater. Some days we are invited to forgive, and forgive again, and we can rise to the challenge. But there can be another kind of day, when I feel my temper rising and my brow lowering. On those days, I try to remember the fact that God has no reason to forgive us and yet he does so, again and again. He chooses to do so because of his grace. Dear Lord, may I always remember that forgiveness is a gift from you, and may I likewise, through your grace, be reminded to exercise forgiveness, joyfully, in my own affairs.

Then Peter said unto them, Repent,
and be baptized every one of you
in the name of Jesus Christ for the remission of sins,
and ye shall receive the gift of the Holy Ghost.

—Acts 2:38

When we forgive, our hearts are lightened. It has taken me much of my adult life to understand that basic premise. And even now, I can approach forgiveness from the standpoint of the gift I'm giving another. It is only after I have forgiven someone, and my spirit lifts, that I remember, again: I benefit as much, if not more, than the person I've pardoned. Dear Lord, thank you for the gift you give freely each time I am moved to absolve another. Thank you for rewarding forgiveness by enriching my heart spiritually.

Dear God, I have been hurt so many times by people, and I am tired of the pain and the anger that is making my life miserable. Please help me find the power within to forgive those who have hurt me and to cut the ties that bind me to those bitter feelings and resentful emotions. I long to be free and at peace, and I know that the only path to peace is forgiveness. Help me be the kind of person who is able to be honorable and noble by forgiving those who have hurt me. It is the hardest thing I have ever done, but with you, nothing is impossible. Amen.

Forgive us, Lord, our sins, for failing to live up to your standards of goodness and justice. We confess our shortcomings. Make us willing to change and help us become persons of godly character. Amen.

Dear Lord and Father of humankind,
Forgive our foolish ways;
Reclothe us in our rightful mind,
In purer lives Thy service find,
In deeper reverence, praise.

—John Greenleaf Whittier

My supreme Lord, give me a forgiving heart. When someone unintentionally ignores me or hurts my feelings, let me respond with forgiveness before they are even aware of the wrong. In these and other situations, I pray that forgiveness will become an automatic response for me—not something I have to consciously work on. I guess what I'm really asking, Lord, is please give me a heart like yours. Only then will I be able to live a life full of spontaneous forgiveness.

God, please forgive those in the world who do not know what they do. Their hearts have grown cold as stone, and they have no love for themselves or for others. I pray for them—these people who do harm to others—that they may somehow find hope and see the light again and that even as they sin and sin again, they will be forgiven. No human is a waste of life, and I ask that the light of your love and compassion melt their hearts and that your mercy and your forgiveness set them free.

Almighty Lord, how can I forgive when the person who has hurt me has shown no remorse? Even though I told him his actions have caused me pain, he refused to admit his wrongdoing. The hurt I feel is like a sack of rocks upon my back, and it slows me and pains me every second of every day. Take this burden from me, and help me recover. Your love is enough to heal any hurt, even those caused by others. If I have your love, I need no one else's. Amen.

Then came Peter to him, and said, Lord,
how oft shall my brother sin against me,
and I forgive him? till seven times?
Jesus saith unto him, I say not unto thee,
Until seven times: but, Until seventy times seven.

—Matthew 18:21–22

My aging parents have required more support in the last year or so, and my brother and I have tried to work together to meet their needs. Most of the time we succeed, but in the past few months, we have started butting heads. Part of our disagreements simply stem from the stress of our current circumstances. Both our parents are very ill and usually conflict occurs when I need to put the needs of my own children first. My brother, who doesn't have a wife or family, doesn't always understand when I need to juggle my caregiving roles. I do the best I can, but I recently found out that my brother has been complaining about me to other family members behind my back. I felt hurt and betrayed. I wish he had come to me to resolve our differences. When I confronted him, we had a heated exchange. I didn't receive an apology, and while I assured him I understood and that we would just move on, I have held bitterness in my heart. That resentment has been eating away at me. Yesterday my wife sat me down. She had guessed at my struggle, and counseled me that if ever there was a time for forgiveness, this was it. My brother and I need one another as we cope with the needs of our parents, and the anger I've been harboring is corrosive to my health and spirit. Dear God, please help me to forgive those who I feel have betrayed me. Please help me move forward with a spirit of grace.

Heaven

In my Father's house are many mansions:
if it were not so, I would have told you.
I go to prepare a place for you.

—John 14:2

When I was a child, I imagined heaven to be an impersonal, abstract place, perhaps filled with fluffy white clouds, and harps, and singing angels. Somehow heaven lacked the comfort and warmth of my own bedroom, with its unique touches. Now that I'm grown, I'm no longer certain of what heaven will be like. Is it a "place" in the sense that I know—a field, or forest, or grassy knoll? Or is it unlike anything I have experienced in this lifetime? I cannot imagine, but heaven feels more personal to me when I remember the biblical promise that there is a spot for me there, which the Lord has prepared! Now I wonder, what personal touches await? Lord, thank you for preparing an individual place for me in heaven.

But none of these things move me, neither count I my life dear unto myself, so that I might finish my course with joy, and the ministry, which I have received of the Lord Jesus, to testify the gospel of the grace of God.

—Acts 20:24

We are products of our environment. I learned from my parents, who learned from their parents, and it is not just what children hear—it is what they see, day in and day out. My parents were good people. They are both deceased, but I believe they are in heaven. I also believe it is my responsibility to live in such a way that carries on their legacy of dignity and grace. I can model that behavior for my own children, teens now, and in so doing inspire them to choose a life informed by Christ's teachings. It is an awesome responsibility to live in such a way that others are inspired to seek the joy of heaven.

For God so loved the world,
that he gave his only begotten Son,
that whosoever believeth in him should not perish,
but have everlasting life.

—John 3:16

I am a hospice nurse, and have seen in my work how the instinct to cling to life is strong. As a Christian, I believe that I can look forward to everlasting life after my time on Earth, but I imagine that when my time does come, it will be hard to let go of the life I know, populated by those I love. It is ironic and yet compelling that we cling to a temporary life on Earth, which is but a glimmer of what eternal life in heaven will be. Lord, help me to appreciate the transient beauty of life on Earth, even as I remember and embrace your promise of heaven and life everlasting.

Nevertheless we, according to his promise,
look for new heavens and a new earth,
wherein dwelleth righteousness.

—2 Peter 3:13

Life can be challenging. It is imperfect. It can be ugly. I commute to work by train, and sometimes the litter I see by the side of the tracks saddens me—papers, plastic bags, abandoned toys, even once the rusted hulk of a car. We are not always good stewards of the world we live in, and while I believe it is important that we continue to try to repair and care for our earthly home, I also take comfort in the assurance of a shining life after this one. "New heavens and a new earth": that promise fills me with hope. Lord, thank you for reminding me that all will be made anew!

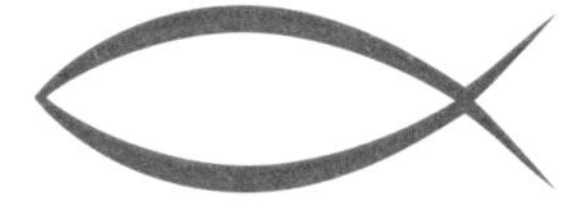

But rather seek ye the kingdom of God;
and all these things shall be added unto you.

—Luke 12:31

Last summer, my wife and I took a road trip out West. We drove from Chicago to Seattle, taking primarily two-lane roads, and making our route up as we went along. I will never forget the evening we pulled into a little town in South Dakota. It was dinnertime, that golden hour when the sunlight looks like thick yellow syrup. As we drove, the fields around us were drenched in a honey-colored light. "This must be what heaven is like," my wife remarked, nodding at a great round lake on the outskirts of town. It almost appeared to be gilded. Her observation filled me with joy—and hope. I was reminded that by setting our sights on God's kingdom, we achieve a blessing in this life.

Sing the wondrous love of Jesus,

Sing his mercy and his grace;

In the mansions bright and blessed,

He'll prepare for us a place.

While we walk the pilgrim pathway,

Clouds will overspread the sky;

But when trav'ling days are over,

Not a shadow, not a sigh.

When we all get to heaven,

What a day of rejoicing that will be!

When we all see Jesus,

We'll sing and shout the victory.

—Eliza E. Hewitt, "When We All Get To Heaven"

Heaven is not reached at a single bound;
But we build the ladder by which we rise
From the lowly earth to the vaulted skies,
And we mount to its summit round by round.

—Josiah Gilbert Holland

When we remember that we are working for the rewards of heaven and not for the praise of people, we are able to press on and persevere in the tasks ahead of us.

But the wisdom that is from above is first pure,
then peaceable, gentle, and easy to be intreated,
full of mercy and good fruits,
without partiality, and without hypocrisy.

—James 3:17

When I read this verse, I realize how perfectly Jesus personified heavenly wisdom. It's a wonder to me that we are called to walk in his footsteps, but then I remember that it is only possible to do it through the Spirit that works in and through us. Thank you, Lord, for making the things of heaven available to those who seek them.

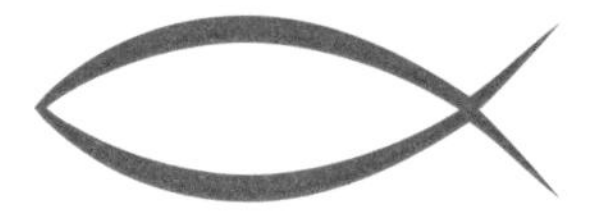

Parenthood

Now his parents went to Jerusalem every year at the feast of the passover.

—Luke 2:41

My wife, two children, and I recently took a road trip to Boston. My middle school son has been studying the American Revolution, and Boston's rich history and wealth of museums drew us. We had a wonderful time exploring the city, but an unanticipated pleasure was the time it took to drive from our Midwestern home to the East Coast and back again. In the car, we read, talked, and listened to music. Upon our return home, we felt refreshed and connected, and my son mentioned that the next time we travel, he hopes we drive again. As he put it: "It'll be our tradition, you know?" The next day we went to church together, and I felt that same connection. Lord, I am reminded of the importance of our family traditions—like going on road trips or worshipping together—and the bonds and continuity they foster. Please grant me the creativity to pursue traditions that enrich my family life; may I never lose sight of their importance.

Lord, behold our family here assembled.

We thank you this place in which we dwell,

for the love that unites us, for the peace accorded us

this day, for the hope with which we expect

the morrow; for the health, the work, the food and the

bright skies that make our lives delightful;

for our friends in all parts of the earth. Amen.

—Robert Louis Stevenson

His parents answered them and said,
We know that this is our son,
and that he was born blind.

—John 9:20

Our friend's daughter has been having problems at school. Because of social and academic challenges the girl faces, her parents have elected to pull her from public school and pursue home schooling. The change mandates major adjustments on the part of the entire family. My friend's wife has quit her job to be at home with their daughter, effecting a change in her own goals and in the family's finances. When my friend shared their decision with me, my knee-jerk reaction—though fortunately I did not voice it—was one of judgment. Public school was good enough for my kids; why wasn't it good enough for this girl? But as my friend and I talked, and I became aware of the emotional difficulties the young woman faces, I began to appreciate the choice my friend and his wife have made, even with its attendant sacrifices. We do what we can to support our children, and people's strengths and needs vary. God, you have blessed me with healthy children, and I thank you. But my kids are human beings, with their own needs, and my wife and I do not hesitate to make the decisions that best support them. Please help me be sensitive to the parents of children with special needs, and respectful of their decisions and life journey.

For this child I prayed; and the Lord hath given me my petition which I asked of him.

—1 Samuel 1:27

Because You Are There

In a silent world, no voice is heard,
No bark of a dog or song of a bird,
No strains of music or chime of a bell;
A noiseless, mysterious place to dwell.

But there is hope in this daunting place,
And happiness comes to a deaf child's face,
When, with his hands, his thoughts he can share,
He has learned to sign, because you are there.

You lift a cloud from the youngster's heart,
And she can smile because you did your part.
You've lightened the load she has to bear.
It isn't as hard, because you are there.

The smile on your face greets them each day.
Your simple gestures chase their fears away.
The love that you give shows them you care.
Their world is better, because you are there.

Children, obey your parents in all things:
for this is well pleasing unto the Lord.

—Colossians 3:20

Dear Lord, I am officially in the "Sandwich Generation," raising my own children while helping my parents navigate the challenges of aging. Mom and Dad, who have always been there for me, now need me in new ways. Dad has developed Parkinson's, and Mom's arthritis is getting worse. My wife and I are devoted to helping them with practical matters like getting to the doctor, cleaning their home, and buying groceries, and I have recently started bringing my older daughter along when we run errands with Mom. The challenges my folks face make me keenly aware of life's cycles of loss and change; I know my daughter feels it, too. But my hope is that these dates with Mom might be a way to demonstrate to my daughter what respect for elders can mean. Aging is a part of being, and compassion is an important lesson. Dear God, help me set the right example for my children through my relationship with my own parents.

Parents lend children their experience and a vicarious memory; children endow their parents with a vicarious immortality.

—George Santayana

God never gives us the light which our children need; he gives it to them.

—Henry Ward Beecher, "Life Thoughts"

Give a little love to a child, and you get a great deal back.

—John Ruskin

By faith Moses, when he was born,
was hid three months of his parents,
because they saw he was a proper child;
and they were not afraid of the king's commandment.

—Hebrews 11:23

Dear Lord, my role as a parent puts me in a commanding position. Children have little power, and it is up to me, as my child's guardian, to be a helpmeet and advocate in a world that is not always just. My son, who is nine, has been dealing with a bully at school. I've had to go in to meet with the principal and the other boy's parents several times, and the parents have on more than one occasion grown belligerent. It's an uncomfortable situation, but I know I must remain strong and level headed in order to support my child. God, please grant me the strength to always do what is right for my child, even at risk of personal discomfort, as the parents of Moses did.

No man can possibly know what life means,
what the world means, until he has a child
and loves it. And then the whole universe changes
and nothing will ever again seem exactly
as it seemed before.

—Lafcadio Hearn

It is not flesh and blood but the heart
which makes us fathers and sons.

—Johann Christoph Friedrich von Schiller

And he arose, and came to his father.
But when he was yet a great way off,
his father saw him, and had compassion,
and ran, and fell on his neck, and kissed him.
And the son said unto him, Father,
I have sinned against heaven, and in thy sight,
and am no more worthy to be called thy son.

—Luke 15:20–21

I love the story of the prodigal son. It reminds me of the bond parents and children share, and it reminds me of the simple fact that our children are human. They are going to make mistakes; sometimes they are going to disappoint us, deeply. But as parents, we are called upon to love our children, and forgive them, even when they have hurt us. (God, I suppose you know exactly what I mean. Even when I make mistakes, your love for me remains a constant.) Dear Lord, may I have the strength and wisdom to always love my children and be there for them, even when they disobey.

Bless our homes, dear God, that we cherish

the daily bread before there is none,

discover each other before we leave

on our separate ways,

and enjoy each other for what we are,

while we have time to do so.

—A Prayer from Hawaii (adapted)

Where we love is home, home that our feet may leave,

but not our hearts. The chain may lengthen,

but it never parts.

—Oliver Wendell Holmes

Stress and Worry

Search me, O God, and know my heart:
try me, and know my thoughts.

—Psalm 139:23

It is not always easy to understand others; it is not always easy to understand oneself! This came home to me last week, when I "woke up on the wrong side of the bed." From the moment I got up to make coffee, I was filled with a pervasive sense of anxiety. I tried to take care, giving myself extra time for my commute to work, and organizing my day to minimize stress. And yet nothing seemed to help until I had the sense to close my office door, put my phone aside, and say the quiet, simple prayer, "Help." I won't tell you that my anxiety magically went away, for it did not. But I had a moment to collect myself, to register some of the things that had piled up throughout the week—a bad grade my son earned in math, the leaky faucet, the fact that I haven't been sleeping as well—and the understanding gave me some context, and consequently some relief. Understanding our own concerns is a part of our ongoing education as to who we are as people. God, you have the power to look into my mind and soul to know what causes my anxiety. Thank you for helping me to remember that. Thank you for being there to guide me.

Heaviness in the heart of man maketh it stoop:
but a good word maketh it glad.

—Proverbs 12:25

We never know what's going on in the life of another person, like the guy who cuts me off in traffic, or the checkout clerk who reacts to a query with impatience. The way someone reacts doesn't always reflect how they feel about me. Instead, it is often a response to the complex circumstances of their life on that given day. God, help me remember to respond to others with grace and kindness—to put good out into the world just for the sake of doing so—because the right words spoken to someone at the right time might lift the worry that burdens another person's heart.

Seeking courage, Lord, I bundle my fears and place them in your hands. Too heavy for me, too weighty even to ponder in this moment, such shadowy terrors shrink to size in my mind and—how wonderful!—wither to nothing in your grasp.

Therefore I say unto you, Take no thought for your life, what ye shall eat, or what ye shall drink; nor yet for your body, what ye shall put on. Is not the life more than meat, and the body than raiment?

—Matthew 6:25

Last weekend, I was busy washing the car, cutting the grass, and taking my good shirts to the dry cleaners. My daughter asked if I might take a break and read with her, and I responded that I had a mile-long list of things to do and no time in which to do them. "We have nice things and I like to keep them nice!" I replied. I felt stressed after we talked, but managed to congratulate myself. After all, I was giving my daughter a good lesson in responsibility and the importance of taking care of our possessions. I even felt proud of how good the car looked as I drove to the cleaners, and started planning what projects in the house I'd tackle upon returning home. But as I drove, it occurred to me—was having a perfectly clean car as important as time with my child? In ten years, when she's gone to college, will it matter that my home was always spotless? I took a breath and retrenched—there were definitely things I needed to accomplish that day, but I understood, suddenly, that time with my kid was important, too—some things could wait. My daughter and I ended up walking to the library when I returned home. We read together there, but also had a good, easy conversation that emerged naturally as we walked. I learned some things about her school week that I doubt she'd have shared if we hadn't had some quality time. House projects? If anything, what I probably need to focus on is streamlining my belongings! God, help me to remember that having too many things can be a source of worry. The more I own, the more I worry about protecting or maintaining. Life is more than material possessions.

Take therefore no thought for the morrow: for the morrow shall take thought for the things of itself. Sufficient unto the day is the evil thereof.

—Matthew 6:34

It's easy to "borrow trouble," even on days when all seems well. This week was a good one—I met a challenging project deadline and received good feedback on the work I'd done. My daughter, who loves music, made it into a prestigious jazz band at school. Our crocuses started blooming, a sure sign that spring is here. And yet, as I poked around the garden, a place that always brings me solace, I found myself worrying about the day when my health might no longer allow me the pleasures I enjoy today. What if my knees give out, as they did for my father, and I can no longer kneel in my garden to plant and weed? What if some day I don't have the stamina to meet tight work deadlines as I do today? Then my daughter came racing outside to join me. She wanted to talk about how to sensitively share news of her acceptance to the jazz band with another friend who did not make the cut. We talked, and our conversation was real and good. My wife poked her head out the door, informing us that she was making a special dinner to celebrate the successful completion of my work project. I let myself be in that moment, and in that moment, I felt joy. God, please help me to stay in the here and now, with its joys and puzzles—not waste my strength on worry about what might happen tomorrow, or in all the days to come.

Lord, I am now in tribulation, and my heart is ill
at ease, for I am much troubled
with the present suffering. . . . Grant me patience,
O Lord, even now in this moment.
Help me, my God, and then I will not fear,
how grievously soever I be afflicted.

—Thomas à Kempis

Casting all your care upon him;
for he careth for you.

—1 Peter 5:7

At work, I manage a team of employees, and it's part of my job to take charge and support those who report to me. Questions? Come to me. Problems? I can help solve them. I take pride in this role, and yet there are times in my own life when I need to remember that I don't have to handle everything. I can—and should—take my problems to God. He actually encourages us to do so because he loves us. Dear Lord, please help me to remember that I can rely on you.

Our Weakness, Your Strength

There is much to drag us back, O Lord:
empty pursuits, trivial pleasures, unworthy cares.
There is much to frighten us away:
pride that makes us reluctant to accept help;
cowardice that recoils from sharing your suffering;
anguish at the prospect of confessing our sins to you.
But you are stronger than all these forces.
We call you our redeemer and saviour because you
redeem us from our empty, trivial existence,
you save us from our foolish fears.
This is your work, which you have completed
and will continue to complete every moment.

—Søren Kierkegaard

Help us, O Lord our God; for we rest on thee,
and in thy name we go against this multitude.
O Lord, thou art our God;
let no man prevail against thee.

—2 Chronicles 14:11

Sometimes the "multitude" we face is a multitude of pain, a multitude of trouble, a multitude of opposition from others, or a multitude of sadness. When it feels as though there is a multitude of something that is too big for us, threatening to distress us, what can we do? There is only one who is bigger and more powerful than anyone or anything else in life. Let us remember today that our God is for us, and his power is greater than that of any multitude.

My Lord and my God, in you I stand today against the multitude that would seek to discourage my faith. In every circumstance that threatens to overwhelm me, please grant me your peace as you exercise your power to protect me.

Aging

For which cause we faint not;
but though our outward man perish,
yet the inward man is renewed day by day.

—2 Corinthians 4:16

I recently turned 50 and have started to see changes in my body. I have had to start watching cholesterol levels. I've had to work harder to stay trim. Sometimes I fear that my mind is not as sharp as it once was. I don't have as great a faculty for remembering things as I did when I was younger, so I rely more on lists to keep the day running smoothly. More and more, conversations with friends circle around to these types of health issues, and sometimes I feel fearful at the prospect of aging. And yet, God reminds us that even when our bodies and minds begin to break down, he renews our spirit. God, thank you for being with me at every age, in every chapter of my life.

The glory of young men is their strength:
and the beauty of old men is the grey head.

—Proverbs 20:29

Yesterday, I looked in the bathroom mirror and noticed some gray hair near my temples, and even the start of what might be a receding hairline. I've never thought of myself as particularly vain, but these changes took me by surprise. I told my wife over breakfast that I'm not sure I like them! I even wondered aloud if I should darken my hair to mask the signs of aging. But as she reminded me, smiling, "God tells us, don't hide our gray—revel in it!" God, thank you for reminding me to take joy in every stage of my life.

Father, you have enriched my life with many identities—son, student, husband, and father. Richness and joy have followed me through each phase of my life, and I have wholeheartedly accepted and enjoyed each role. But you knew, didn't you, Lord, that the title of father would make such a strong claim on my heart? How I praise you for the greatest of your gifts, my children, and for the fulfillment they have brought. I need no other affirmation than to be called father. My children have taught me to forget myself, and through them, I have learned what it means to be your child.

The righteous shall flourish like the palm tree:
he shall grow like a cedar in Lebanon.
Those that be planted in the house of the Lord
shall flourish in the courts of our God.
They shall still bring forth fruit in old age;
they shall be fat and flourishing.

—Psalm 92:12–14

When I was a boy, I had a close relationship with my father's father, a quiet, righteous man who had a little house in northern Michigan. My parents and I would go up to see him every summer, and during our visits, I'd take long walks with my grandfather. We didn't always talk, but we shared one another's company with pleasure. As I became a teen, though, I was drawn more and more to my friends. One summer I told my parents that I didn't want to make the yearly trip. I was old enough to stay home alone, I argued, and preferred to remain behind. I still remember my dad's response: "There will come a day when your grandpa is no longer with us. He has much to offer, and you will be glad of the times you shared when he is gone." I reluctantly agreed. It turned out that visit was an especially good one. My grandfather taught me how to play chess, and though he had started to walk with a cane, we still hiked the property. We enjoyed our usual companionable silence on the walk. I returned home feeling restored. The following winter, a heart attack took my grandfather's life. To this day, I feel tremendous gratitude that I shared that last special visit with a man whose decency continues to inform who I strive to be.

Thou shalt rise up before the hoary head,
and honour the face of the old man, and fear thy God:
I am the Lord.

—Leviticus 19:32

I live in a time and society that worship youth: open any magazine and there are ads for products that help us to "stay young and beautiful." We strive for youth even as—perhaps because—we live in a culture that can marginalize elders as irrelevant, or a burden. Unattractive. This attitude sometimes makes me fear aging. I also find myself fighting the impulse to pull back from the elderly people in my life, again, out of fear—fear of their vulnerability, of their bumps and spots and rough places. But God reminds us that when we honor our elders, we honor God. Dear Lord, help me to keep my heart focused on what matters, not age, or appearance, but the humanity in others, as well as the humanity in myself. Teach me to remember that true beauty comes from where our body and spirit meet.

Hearken unto thy father that begat thee,
and despise not thy mother when she is old.

—Proverbs 23:22

Throughout my life I have enjoyed many milestones: attaining a college degree, securing my first job, marriage, the birth of my two children, and just recently, seeing my relationship with my parents flip as they age and begin to rely on me as I once relied on them. Each life chapter has brought its joys and trials, and while it is my privilege to support my mom and dad, I confess that their new vulnerability sometimes fills me with fear, and on my worst days, resentment. My life is so full. My children, in high school now, still need me, perhaps more than ever as they face more adult challenges of their own. Sometimes I feel as though there are not enough hours in the day to work and make sure the needs of my loved ones are met. Sometimes I don't want to face or be present for the way my parents have aged. God, as I grow older and my life becomes more complicated, please help me to remember to always honor my mother and father. They remain my parents and have much to offer me. May I never forget them or shirk my responsibilities amid the everyday cares of working and parenting.

Let me but live my life from year to year,
With forward face and unreluctant soul;
Not hurrying to, nor turning from, the goal;
Not mourning for the things that disappear
In the dim past, nor holding back in fear
From what the future veils; but with a whole
And happy heart, that pays its toll
To Youth and Age, and travels on with cheer.

—Henry Van Dyke

Lord, you know better than I know myself
that I am growing older, and will some day be old...

Release me from craving to straighten out
everybody's affairs... With my vast store
of wisdom it seems a pity not to use it all,
but you know that I want a few friends at the end.

...seal my lips on my own aches and pains—
they are increasing, and my love of rehearsing
this is becoming sweeter as the years go by...

Keep me reasonably sweet. I do not want
to be a saint—some of them are so hard
to live with—but a sour old woman is one of
the crowning works of the devil.

—Anonymous

Lord, today I ask your special blessing on the elderly among us. No matter how old we are, we notice our bodies aging. How difficult it must be to be near the end of life and struggling to hold on to mobility, vision, hearing, and wellness of being. Give us compassion for those older than we are, Lord, and thank you for your promise that you will be with us to the very end of our days.

Generosity

And when she had done giving him drink, she said,
I will draw water for thy camels also,
until they have done drinking.

—Genesis 24:19

Life is busy. And sometimes I am so caught up in the demands of the day (get the kids to school, work, pick up the dry cleaning) that I forget the importance of slowing down and favoring generosity of spirit over efficiency. Just yesterday, I was racing through the grocery store; I'd promised my wife I'd pick up some meat for dinner, and as I rushed down the aisle I heard someone call my name. It was my daughter's kindergarten teacher, an older lady who, even standing on tiptoe, barely clears my shoulder. She smiled at me and asked if I could reach up and grab a few cans from the top shelf. My first reaction, which I hope I suppressed, was annoyance; I was in a hurry, after all! But I stopped, and this lady was so grateful, and she complimented my daughter (which of course endeared me to her), so that I was still warmed by the encounter as I paid for my groceries. I even felt inspired to crack a joke with the bagger, a raw-faced kid I'd never noticed before, and when I got home, I made a point of asking my daughter about school—I even invited her to "help" me unpack the groceries. Five-year-olds aren't very efficient, but the time we shared was worth far more than an orderly fridge. I reflected later how those encounters and the mindful connection they provided filled my own spirit. Opening myself to generosity can be like cracking open a door on stiff hinges, but once I do, and the light shines in, it gets easier and easier to throw the door wide to more opportunity. God, help me remember that one generous act begets another. Help me remember to take that first step, because when I do, I benefit as much as those to whom I've reached out.

Dear Lord, generosity is your way, and I seek to emulate your goodness when I help others—when I give of my time and energy and resources. It feels good to give of myself—giving draws upon my best self—and when I do so, please be with me. Remind me not to become puffed up in pride about my acts of generosity. Remind me not to call attention to what I have done. I give for you, and to lift others up, not to make myself look good.

He doth execute the judgment of the fatherless and widow, and loveth the stranger, in giving him food and raiment.

—Deuteronomy 10:18

When I was a boy, my Sunday School teacher encouraged us, one week, to keep track of the kind things we did for others. I prepared a careful ledger, describing the dishes I washed for my mom after dinner, and the popcorn I shared with my younger brother. The next Sunday, I proudly showed my list to the teacher. He praised my efforts, which pleased me greatly. I looked up to this man the way I looked up to my own father. We talked about how important it is to do kindnesses for the ones we love, and then he said, "And the next step, son, is to serve those we don't even know!" He explained that while it takes just that little bit more effort to extend ourselves for strangers, that is Christ's way. Dear Lord, all these years later, those words have stayed with me; may I be generous to strangers, not just to those I know and love.

All our opportunities, abilities, and resources come from God. They are given to us to hold in sacred trust for him. Cooperating with God will permit us to generously pass on to others some of the many blessings from his rich storehouse.

Lord, grant me a simple, kind, open, believing,
loving and generous heart,
worthy of being your dwelling place.

—John Sergieff

We all have numerous resources from which to share. Having a "generous spirit" does not mean simply giving money. Time is another precious commodity, and generous volunteers enable many organizations to function well—hospitals, schools, missions, animal shelters, community centers, nursing homes, child-care centers, churches—the list goes on. Look around. What do you have to share? A "spirit of generosity" means open-handedly giving time, energy, and creativity, as well as monetary resources. Great is the reward of the man who generously gives whatever he has to help others.

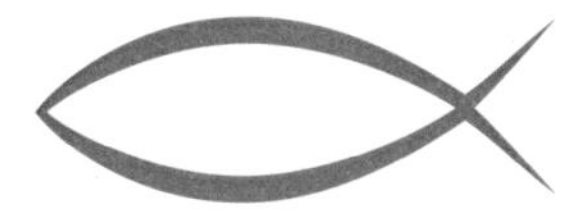

I exhort therefore, that, first of all, supplications, prayers, intercessions, and giving of thanks, be made for all men.

—1 Timothy 2:1

Dear Lord, I live in a time and place of entitlement. Sometimes, when others are kind to me, generously offering their time or assistance, I am in such a hurry that I take their kindness as no more than my due. My neighbor set aside his own work to help me when I struggled in building a prefab kitchen island equipped with hard-to-decipher directions. My sister took off work and traveled far to attend my son's middle school graduation. Now I have a sturdy piece of furniture, and my son's day was enriched by the presence and support of his aunt. God, these acts of love deserve to be recognized as such. Please help me to remember to slow down, appreciate, and thank those who are generous to me.

Every man according as he purposeth in his heart, so let him give; not grudgingly, or of necessity: for God loveth a cheerful giver.

—2 Corinthians 9:7

My wife is a nurse, and lately the hospital where she works has been short-staffed. Though new hires will soon be brought on board, for the time being, my wife's schedule is more taxing. When I promised her I would pick up the slack at home, including taking on more of the cooking and cleaning, I was sincere. And yet, yesterday I was tired and ungraciously reminded my wife of all I was doing. Her face fell, and I was ashamed. Here we are, both working so hard, and I spoiled my kind efforts with bitterness! I have since made amends, but dear Lord, please remind me to give with good cheer, not grumbling.

Joy

And these things write we unto you,
that your joy may be full.

—1 John 1:4

My mother was a joyful person. She faced challenges like everyone else—her health in particular troubled her off and on through most of her adult life—but as a rule, she chose to focus on the positive. Her joyful outlook took many forms—she was a calm, good listener; she embraced new experiences; she was interested and interesting. And something that strikes me now is how her radiant spirit was often contagious. I myself would sometimes return from school glum or discouraged, but if we spent some quiet time together—working in the garden, say, or sometimes I would finish my homework in the kitchen while Mom cooked dinner—my own spirits lifted. Mom died last year, and as an adult, I am left to carry her bright torch for my own family. God, help me to always remember how important it is to share our joy with others so that they may experience it.

But the fruit of the Spirit is love, joy, peace, longsuffering, gentleness, goodness, faith.

—Galatians 5:22

As an adult with many demands on my time and energy, I am always interested in how to consistently achieve my potential and be my best self. For many years, I've enjoyed swimming as a way to stay healthy, both physically and emotionally. After a long day, a good swim clears my head, tones my muscles, and keeps me sharp and upbeat. Similarly, I've found that staying spiritually active has a positive affect on my outlook. Like exercise, staying spiritually engaged takes discipline—and sometimes I would rather just sit on the couch and eat chips!

But when I make the effort, physical and spiritual exercise helps me to realize joy. Lord, please may I always remember that happiness can be part of the package when I develop my spiritual muscle. I can work at making joy a constant in my life.

When we think of joy, we often think of things that are new—a new day, a new baby, a new love, a new beginning, the promise of a new home with God in heaven. Rejoicing in these things originates with having joy in the God who makes all things new. Rather than relying on earthly pleasures to provide happiness, the scriptures command that we rejoice in God and in each new day he brings. Joy is a celebration of the heart that goes beyond circumstances to the very foundation of joy—the knowledge that God loves us.

Hitherto have ye asked nothing in my name: ask, and ye shall receive, that your joy may be full.

—John 16:24

Being an adult—perhaps more specifically being a spiritual adult—does not mean that we have to be dull or unadventurous. Recently, I was happily reminded of this fact when I met a woman at my church who embodies the spirit of adventure. Like me, Liz is probably in her late 50s. Like me, she lost her spouse to terminal illness. I have admittedly become stuck in my ways since becoming a widower five years ago. Meeting Liz has been like a shot of sunshine. She is taking lessons to earn a motorcycle license. She loves working in clay and has sold her pottery at local craft fairs. Though she still holds down a full-time job, Liz enjoys volunteering at a nearby animal shelter, an effort that has brought two sleek and satisfied tabby cats into her life. I don't know where our friendship will lead, but I can say that my relationship with Liz has broadened my horizons and filled me with joy. God, thank you for reminding me that you want us to be happy.

Joy will always return to those who love God. We may find ourselves brought low by some of life's difficulties—and certainly by the tragedies that take us by storm. But none of these—not even the tragedies—can rob us of the deep-seated joy we have in our God. "Weeping may endure for a night, but joy cometh in the morning." (Psalm 30:5). We may weep, even as Jesus did at times, but like him, we have a future joy set before us that no struggle on this earth can undermine or destroy. Our morning lies just ahead.

A merry heart doeth good like a medicine:
but a broken spirit drieth the bones.

—Proverbs 17:22

Last summer I started bicycling regularly for my health. One day late in August I jumped a curb too exuberantly, wiped out, and broke my leg. Fortunately, I work from home, so my schedule was not too affected during my recuperation time. And yet, because I am by nature an active person, the limitations of my injury—not to mention the bulky cast—put a real cramp in my style. I'll confess that some days I felt down. My good friends Dave and Sara were a lifeline during this time. They'd stop by to watch movies, bring in dinner, or just hang out. We laughed a lot during these visits and I invariably found that after they looked in on me, my mood soared and I felt better overall. Long after my leg has healed, I remember their kindness with gratitude. Lord, thank you for the friends and loved ones who uplift me. Just as exercise, being joyful is good for my health!

And ye now therefore have sorrow:
but I will see you again, and your heart shall rejoice,
and your joy no man taketh from you.

—John 16:22

Life has its difficult chapters. In the past two years, both my parents died and my beloved son struggled with his coursework, to the point where he had to take a break from university. He suffered through a period of confusion and depression, and is still not sure if he will in fact return to school. It's been a hard time for my family, and yet amid the challenges, I have enjoyed the support of my wife and a tightly knit group of friends, one of whom helped my son get a job that allows him to be self-reliant while he decides on next steps. My life isn't "perfect," and yet each morning I wake to a choice—how can I embrace what is good in this day? How can I tap into God within me, no matter what else transpires? Lord, help me remember that external circumstances cannot define my joy. Rather, joy is something I can nurture within, even as I, and those I love, experience ups and downs.

Lord, you are the source of all joy! Regardless of how happy we may feel at any given time, we know happiness is fleeting. Happiness, so dependent on temporary circumstances, is fickle and unpredictable. But joy in you is forever! And so we come to you today, Lord, rejoicing in all you were, all you are, and all you will ever be. Because of you, we rejoice!

Joy is the echo of God's life within us.

—Joseph Marmion

There is joy in being in God's presence. There is no other place we find joy in its fullness, shimmering in all its facets, except in the presence of God himself. "Thou wilt shew me the path of life," said the psalmist. "In thy presence is fulness of joy; at thy right hand there are pleasures for evermore" (Psalm 16:11). We can try manufacturing our own versions of joy by pursuing some of life's temporary pleasures—achievements, recreation, entertainment, material possessions, and such. But these don't come close to the rarified joy we experience when we draw close to our heavenly Father so we can spend time in his presence.

Joy is not gush; joy is not jolliness.
Joy is perfect acquiescence in God's will
because the soul delights in God himself.

—H. W. Webb-Peploe

When I think of God, my heart is so full of joy
that the notes leap and dance as they leave my pen:
and since God has given me a cheerful heart,
I serve him with a cheerful spirit.

—Franz Joseph Haydn

Materialism and Wealth

But if any provide not for his own,
and specially for those of his own house,
he hath denied the faith, and is worse than an infidel.

—1 Timothy 5:8

When my stepfather died, he left a sum of money to me. I was surprised and at first a little overwhelmed, but after a brief period of what I can only call dazed euphoria, my wife and I consulted with a financial planner. We wanted to be wise stewards of this unexpected income. After our meeting with the advisor, we determined that we would use a large portion of the money for our daughter's college education, and then put aside the rest for retirement. Because of health concerns I've been facing, it is important to me to know that my wife will have money to draw upon in the likely event that I die before she does. God, wealth gives me an obligation to provide for my family. I am grateful for the means to do so.

Okay, Lord, I know "it's only stuff," but much of it is useful, and I want to take good care of it. Help me see the line between wanting to be a good steward and caring too much about material things. That line is often blurry from my earthly perspective. Help me be a responsible caretaker without putting too much value on mere "stuff."

Lord, if only all the false gods that lure us were clearly labeled. We are introduced to worldly ambition, wealth, physical perfection—any number of attractive enticements—and it isn't until we realize that the pursuit of them is using up way too much of our resources that we discover we have made these things our gods. Forgive us, Lord. Help us to keep even good things in balance and never to pursue anything with more fervor than we pursue our relationship with you.

Prosperity is only an instrument to be used, not a deity to be worshipped.

—Calvin Coolidge

Let your conversation be without covetousness;
and be content with such things as ye have:
for he hath said, I will never leave thee,
nor forsake thee.

—Hebrews 13:5

My wife has become friendly with some of the other parents at our son's school, and we were recently invited to a barbecue hosted by one of her new acquaintances. When we arrived the night of the event, I saw that the house was a very large, modern house, probably worth three times the price of our modest ranch-style home. I felt a twinge of envy, only exacerbated when the host, a cheerful, bluff man, invited me downstairs to see the movie theater he'd had built, and a custom wine cellar. I got through the evening by smiling mechanically. I could only imagine what my wife was thinking. Did she wish we lived in this type of house? Did she envy the host's wife, who had a state-of-the-art kitchen? Later that night, as we wound down before bed, my wife noted, "They are really nice people. But gosh, that house is so big! It seemed a little impersonal, you know? I prefer our messy little house; it seems like home!" Dear God, protect me from envying what others have, when my own life is so rich!

For all that is in the world, the lust of the flesh, and the lust of the eyes, and the pride of life, is not of the Father, but is of the world.

—1 John 2:16

I recently had lunch with an old college friend, Dan, who always lifts my spirits when we get together. I was excited to share that we've recently purchased a new car. With my youngest daughter out of college, we enjoy a little more disposable income, and so my wife and I splurged on a vehicle loaded with extras. I could tell my friend was happy for me, but as I returned to the car in conversation again and again, I noticed

Dan's eyes starting to glaze over. That gave me pause, and I had enough sense to switch gears. I asked about the mission work Dan will be doing in the coming year. Dan, in turn, asked about my daughter's graduation, and our lunch got back on track. I parted from my friend feeling restored, and thankful I'd caught myself before our time together was soured by too much focus on possessions. Lord, thank you for reminding me that it's okay to enjoy material things, but they are just that—things. Being fixated on belongings is not what God wants.

Lord, you know how much time and effort I put into surrounding myself with my favorite things. Sometimes I wonder if it's always worth it. Please help me sort out what's truly valuable and what I can do without. One thing I know is worth pursuing is the wisdom found in your Word. As I read it and your Spirit helps me to comprehend it, I feel rich indeed.

He that loveth silver shall not be satisfied with silver; nor he that loveth abundance with increase: this is also vanity.

—Ecclesiastes 5:10

For a period of years, I enjoyed a high-powered job with a significant income. I enjoyed the perks money can buy—a nice house, a good car, and designer clothing. But looking back, I can see that I labored under the misconception that possessions would bring me lasting satisfaction. Unfortunately, that was not the case. Soon after I bought and furnished my home, it occurred to me how nice it would be to have a second home. I loved my car until a colleague got a newer, improved model. I spent a lot of time just maintaining my possessions—taking the car in to be washed and detailed, hiring people to keep the houses clean—and many days, I felt dissatisfied. It was only when I made the decision to simplify my life, to divest myself of some of the possessions that were taking up so much of my time and focus instead on matters of substance, including my relationships with others and my own spirituality, that I gained some measure of peace. The problem with money and acquisition is there is no end—no level of satisfaction. God, help me to stay focused on what really matters.

Lay not up for yourselves treasures upon earth,
where moth and rust doth corrupt,
and where thieves break through and steal:
But lay up for yourselves treasures in heaven,
where neither moth nor rust doth corrupt,
and where thieves do not break through nor steal:
For where your treasure is, there will your heart be also.

—Matthew 6:19–21

When my wife and I were first married, we were what I think is sometimes called "house proud": we would spend weeks looking for just the right couch. Even a dish drainer was chosen after great deliberation. We put a lot of energy into making our home look a certain way, and we took pride in our possessions. Then my wife got pregnant. When our daughter was born, the "look" of the house was sometimes sacrificed for the practicalities of baby accoutrements. As our daughter grew, we adopted two cats. That couch we chose with such care has taken quite a beating. With kids and pets running around, the house isn't quite the showplace we nurtured 10 years ago. But it's a happy home, filled with artwork and books and love. Sometimes things break. Sometimes things get torn or stained. It doesn't seem to matter the way it once did. Thank you, God, for helping me to learn where my treasure truly lies.

But godliness with contentment is great gain.
For we brought nothing into this world,
and it is certain we can carry nothing out.
And having food and raiment
let us be therewith content.

—1 Timothy 6:6–8

Content with just food and clothing? Really, Lord? I'm thankful that you provide for my basic needs, but there's much, much more on my wish list. Sometimes I act like I'm entitled to certain things—a well-paying job for little effort on my part, minimal traffic on the way to said job, restaurant lunches every day, and seamless relationships with loved ones. Help me to be thankful for the countless blessings in my life and to always be ready to help others rather than focusing on adding to my own stores. Please guide me, Lord. I'm ready to answer your call to contentment.

Relationships

He that covereth a transgression seeketh love;
but he that repeateth a matter separateth very friends.

—Proverbs 17:9

I have a flexible job that allows me to work at home, but a couple days a week, I drive in to the office. I like my co-workers, but because I don't see them every day, I feel the need to work harder to stay connected with them. Staying connected is a worthy goal, but lately I've developed a tendency to draw others close via gossip and sardonic commentary on other colleagues. Wanting to "get the dirt" on others is a human tendency, and I've exploited that, leavening my observations with humor so as to come across in what I've liked to think is a likable fashion. In fact, I took pride in my reputation for being caustic and funny, until the other day, when a new hire approached me and said, only half joking, "I hear I need to stay on your good side!"

Her comment made me see myself in a different light, and I feel compelled to make some changes in my approach to the workplace. Dear Lord, teach me the wisdom of exercising good judgment and not gossiping about the shortcomings of others.

Wealth maketh many friends;
but the poor is separated from his neighbour.

—Proverbs 19:4

Lord, I live in an increasingly tiered society, in which people associate only with others of similar income. I am grateful to be solidly middle class, with all the opportunity that affords me and my family, and I take pride in my ability to provide for my loved ones. Yet I must remember not to let economics alone inform my relationships with others. The type of car I drive or the size of my home are hollow gauges for who I am as a person. To judge or be judged based on this criteria is not only shallow, but foolhardy. God, help me to remember to choose my friends wisely, honoring the qualities that matter—integrity, creativity, wisdom, sense of justice, and kindness—rather than a person's wealth or status.

And as ye would that men should do to you,
do ye also to them likewise.

—Luke 6:31

Yesterday I got into a car accident. It was my fault—I was in a hurry and tried to cross an intersection just as yellow turned to red—but I felt defensive and berated the driver whose car I had clipped. I was embarrassed when the driver met my bluster with calm grace. Later, after I'd regained my composure, it also struck me how much I appreciated being spoken to respectfully, though I myself had been less than gracious. The other driver's consideration made an impression, and when I told my wife about it, she smiled gently and observed, "That guy was probably just treating you the way he wished you'd treat him!" God, remind me to treat others as I would want them to treat me.

And the things that thou hast heard of me among many witnesses, the same commit thou to faithful men, who shall be able to teach others also.

—2 Timothy 2:2

Lord, I have the conviction that your presence in my life makes it better. When I let you into my heart, you inform the way I treat others, the way I approach work, the way I move through my days. And good things are meant to be shared! God, help me to share with others the good wisdom I have learned from you. I don't have to proselytize—that's not my style. But through my actions I can demonstrate my beliefs, and in this way create a ripple effect—good begetting good begetting good, with results far beyond what I might even be able to comprehend.

And they continued stedfastly in the apostles' doctrine and fellowship, and in breaking of bread, and in prayers.

—Acts 2:42

When I was a boy, my mom used to talk about "refilling the well," by which she meant the joy she took in being with people who filled her up—who restored her. I thought of her expression last week, when I had lunch with an old classmate. When he and I parted, I was struck by how being with this friend energized rather than depleted me. He is a calm, spiritual person, and our times together never fail to leave me feeling uplifted. Our conversations are wide-ranging and thoughtful, and my friend is a person with whom I feel comfortable sharing my spiritual musings. He and I challenge one another. We don't always agree, but our relationship is such that we inspire one another to learn and grow. Lord, may I remember the importance of developing relationships with other believers, whose fellowship and spiritual life can help to deepen my faith.

Fret not thyself because of evildoers, neither be thou envious against the workers of iniquity. For they shall soon be cut down like the grass, and wither as the green herb. Commit thy way unto the Lord; trust also in him; and he shall bring it to pass.

—Psalm 37:1–2, 5

Please, Lord, step into this situation. I don't know what to do. Things were done, words were said, and now I'm at odds with someone. Maybe I was wrong, but I don't think so. Honestly, I want to blame the other person for all of it, but maybe I have a blind spot. I want to sort things out and turn things around, but I'm not sure where to start. I don't know if a half-baked apology will do any good, especially if I don't really mean it. And actually, I should be receiving an apology, but I doubt that will ever happen. I beg you, please do your work here. Shine your light so we see things clearly. Use your power to dismantle whatever grudges we have piled up. I commit this whole mess to you.

And let us not be weary in well doing: for in due season we shall reap, if we faint not. As we have therefore opportunity, let us do good unto all men, especially unto them who are of the household of faith.

—Galatians 6:9–10

I'll admit it, dear Lord, sometimes I do get weary. I try to show your love to others—by being caring, by giving, and by going the extra mile. But those extra miles add up. There are a lot of people who take advantage of my kindness. They assume I won't mind doing some extra work, giving them a ride, or rescheduling my life around theirs. That's just the way I am. But I have to tell you, Lord, I'm tired of it. Please give me some extra strength soon, or I'm just going to shut down. Please help me!

Let your conversation be without covetousness; and be content with such things as ye have: for he hath said, I will never leave thee, nor forsake thee. So that we may boldly say, The Lord is my helper, and I will not fear what man shall do unto me.

—Hebrews 13:5–6

Anyone who has ever been abandoned deeply fears that they will be abandoned again. Often the worm of insecurity eats away at subsequent relationships, weakening and eventually destroying them. This, in turn, feeds the existing fear. It's a cycle of destruction that has no cure in human relationships, for even if our loved ones are faithful, still they are mortal. That's why God's promise to never leave or forsake us is such a powerful assurance. When we lay hold of it even with a seed of faith, over time God's unfailing presence causes our seedling faith to grow up into an unshakable oak of security.

Father, how I need the security of your presence! You are truly the only one who can say that you will never abandon me. For you will be with me always—in life, in death, and in the life to come.

Serving Others

As every man hath received the gift,
even so minister the same one to another,
as good stewards of the manifold grace of God.

—1 Peter 4:10

It is easier to serve others when my own life is going well. During those chapters in life when things are more or less on an even keel, I am filled with cheer, and I go out into the world wanting to share that goodwill. The act of service comes less easily to me when life presents challenges. When burdened by stress at work, say, or the struggles my son periodically faces from bullies at school, my tendency is to look inward. God, teach me to strive to help others no matter what is going on in my life. You serve us regardless of externals. Service is a gift from you! Remembering this puts me in the right frame of mind to serve others.

I long to help every needy person in the world, Lord. Perhaps the most effective way to do this is by praying that you will send help wherever it is needed. Meanwhile, there is my corner of the universe with its many needs, and some of these are surely within my reach: half of my sandwich to the person standing near the freeway ramp with a sign; an evening spent going through my closet and setting aside items to donate; a weekend afternoon of helping with events at my church; a monthly visit to the sick, homebound, or imprisoned. It's a privilege to honor you by extending your compassion—in person.

Love is others oriented. Jesus' example has shown us what true love is like: "Hereby perceive we the love of God, because he laid down his life for us: and we ought to lay down our lives for the brethren" (1 John 3:16). Each time we set aside our druthers to see to someone else's best interest, we're exercising that others-oriented kind of love that Jesus demonstrated. And since our motivation for self-sacrifice is out of kindness and compassion (rather than compulsion or any form of fear), the joy in giving makes each personal sacrifice well worthwhile.

If we are devoted to the cause of humanity,
we shall soon be crushed and broken-hearted,
for we shall often meet with more ingratitude
from men than we would from a dog;
but if our motive is love to God,
no ingratitude can hinder us
from serving our fellow men.

—Oswald Chambers

One of the principle rules of religion is
to lose no occasion of serving God.
And since he is invisible to our eyes,
we are to serve him in our neighbor,
which he receives as if done to himself in person,
standing visibly before us.

—John Wesley

I have shewed you all things, how that so labouring ye ought to support the weak, and to remember the words of the Lord Jesus, how he said, It is more blessed to give than to receive.

—Acts 20:35

I am grateful for the blessings in my life: a strong marriage, good health, and a steady job. I firmly believe that these advantages put me in a position to help those less fortunate than myself. On a fundamental level, I think that's why we're here—to assist others. But some days I do grow weary of the work constant service (either service I've elected to do or that has been thrust upon me) requires. On those days, God, please help me to remember how giving fills one spiritually. Christ taught that it is better to give than to receive; please help me to remember this on the days that I struggle.

For, brethren, ye have been called unto liberty;
only use not liberty for an occasion to the flesh,
but by love serve one another.
For all the law is fulfilled in one word, even in this;
Thou shalt love thy neighbour as thyself.

—Galatians 5:13–14

I am grateful to live in a democratic society where I can live freely and do as I please. I have a steady job, which consequently allows me to pursue multiple interests that include travel and food. I thoroughly enjoy exploring new cuisines, for example, and cooking for and eating out with friends. I feel lucky to be free to engage in such rewarding experiences—they "fill me up"—yet I also know that reaching out to others is an important part of becoming a fulfilled, evolved person. To that end, I recently signed up to volunteer with Meals on Wheels. I have already met some cool seniors, folks I likely would never have encountered in my usual orbit. I find myself looking forward to my interactions with them each week. God, help me to honor the freedom I enjoy by helping others, not just by indulging myself.

So after he had washed their feet,
and had taken his garments, and was set down again,
he said unto them, Know ye what I have done to you?
Ye call me Master and Lord: and ye say well;
for so I am. If I then, your Lord and Master,
have washed your feet;
ye also ought to wash one another's feet.

—John 13:12–14

As a parent of two little girls, I am deeply aware of how my children learn—not just from what I say, but what I do. Jesus set the example of service, and I try to set a good example of service for my children's sake. Every week, I take the kids to volunteer at a local animal shelter. I think it's good for my daughters to see their dad cheerfully and voluntarily offering time and effort to a cause he believes in, and it's something the three of us share every week. "It feels good to do something good, doesn't it?" my daughter said the other day. I feel happy for her that she's coming to that realization at a relatively young age. God, thank you for my children. Thank you for helping me to teach them to put good out into the world.

Lord, today I pray for all those who are in desperate need of help in order to survive: victims of earthquakes and tornadoes, the homeless, and the physically and emotionally destitute people of our world. Make yourself known to them, Lord. May they all see that their true help comes only from you! You who created them will not leave them without help, nor without hope.

My little children, let us not love in word, neither in tongue; but in deed and in truth.

—1 John 3:18

Actions speak louder than words. To tell someone we love them is a good thing, but to serve another person is profound. Service is an act of love, and every time I help my children with their homework; or surprise my wife by cooking dinner; or comfort a friend who is facing loss by sending a card or spending quiet time with them, I am not only telling, I am showing them my love. Dear God, help me to always remember to back up what I say by what I do.

In charity there is no excess.

—Francis Bacon

Wisdom

If any of you lack wisdom, let him ask of God, that giveth to all men liberally, and upbraideth not; and it shall be given him.

—James 1:5

I recently took on a new position at work. It's a stretch for me, and while I welcome the change (my previous duties no longer challenged me), I am also fearful of failure. My new position will require a steep learning curve, and demands that I oversee a number of employees. What if I can't master the material? What if I don't have what it takes to manage others wisely? But I must remember that God is always there to help me. He can increase wisdom—not just spiritually, but in all ways. Dear Lord, please be with me as I challenge myself to develop intellectually and master new skills. Please help me to stay sharp, and to grow as a person, with energy and grace.

The way of a fool is right in his own eyes:
but he that hearkeneth unto counsel is wise.

—Proverbs 12:15

I am what they call a "self-made man." Right out of college, I started a little company with friends, and in only a few years, the enterprise has grown successful. My position requires that I manage a team of employees. My strategy has traditionally been a "tough love" approach. Not long ago, I was visiting my parents and my dad heard my interactions with an employee over the phone. Later that evening, he brought up the phone call and counseled me to soften my approach. "You've got to keep a light touch," he advised, and I immediately felt defensive. My business was doing well! It was my job to keep the others in line! And yet upon reflection, I remembered that my dad has a lifetime of experience to draw upon. Over the years, he has been respected—even loved—by those who report to him. Though I didn't want to hear it at the time, maybe he does have something to share.

Dear Lord, help me to remember that wisdom comes from listening to others.

With the ancient is wisdom; and in length of days understanding. With him is wisdom and strength, he hath counsel and understanding.

—Job 12:12–13

My parents died when I was a young man, barely out of school, and at first, I proceeded through life almost blindly. I made my way as best I could, but sometimes it was a lonely road. I have learned in the years since that God puts people into my path, to help guide me, and when I remain open, I can benefit from the knowledge others have to share. Many of these folks are older than me. They possess the wisdom born of experience, and a broad worldview that helps me to keep perspective. Dear Lord, please may I always remember to seek instruction from those who have gone down the path before me.

He that hath knowledge spareth his words:
and a man of understanding is of an excellent spirit.

—Proverbs 17:27

When I was a young man, I felt invincible. I didn't think there was anything anyone else could teach me. Like many young men before me, I delighted in pontificating and boasting to anyone who might hear. In retrospect, I see that I mistook saying something for actually having something to say! At my first real job, I came under the supervision of a quiet, much older man. He was clearly respected by his peers, and yet he spoke little. During meetings, he'd listen quietly. When he did speak, everyone paid attention. As time went on, I began to want to emulate his style, and so I asked him about it. "Don't talk until you really have something to say," he counseled. "And by listening, you'll learn a lot in the meantime." His words have stayed with me. God, please always help me remember that to learn, I am wise to speak less and listen more.

The heart of the prudent getteth knowledge;
and the ear of the wise seeketh knowledge.

—Proverbs 18:15

My wife and I had our first and only child, Amanda, later in life, and honestly, that child has been a gift in ways I never could have anticipated. One way our daughter has enriched my life is that, truly, she keeps me learning and growing. Amanda has such diverse interests. Through her, I've been introduced to anime movies, and new styles of music. She has even gotten me interested in the works of Edgar Allan Poe! These are areas I had never explored previously, and I appreciate being able to experience them with my child. Thank you, God, for the gift of a child who reminds me to never stop learning. May I always be a student of life.

Knowledge stops at the edge of the earth.

Faith goes beyond the stars, illimitable,

calm, all-comprehending.

The wisdom of the world is a surface

wisdom and breeds only a surface humor.

The wisdom of faith reaches

from heaven to hell,

into the heart of all living;

and when it smiles

the angels of God smile with it.

—Reverend F. X. Lasance